THE ONE-TWO PUNCH BOXING WORKOUT

12 WEEKS TO KNOCK-OUT FITNESS

★ ANDY DUMAS ★
JAMIE SOMERVILLE

Contemporary Books

Chicago   New York   San Francisco   Lisbon   London   Madrid   Mexico City
Milan   New Delhi   San Juan   Seoul   Singapore   Sydney   Toronto

Library of Congress Cataloging-in-Publication Data

Dumas, Andy.
    The one-two punch boxing workout : 12 weeks to knock-out fitness /
Andy Dumas and Jamie Somerville.
        p.   cm.
    ISBN 0-8092-9323-4
    1. Boxing—Training.   2. Physical fitness.   I. Somerville, Jamie.
II. Title.

GV1137.6 D86   2001
613.7′11—dc21   2001028027

Contemporary Books

A Division of The McGraw·Hill Companies

1 2 3 4 5 6 7 8 9 0   VLP/VLP   0 9 8 7 6 5 4 3 2 1

ISBN 0-8092-9323-4

This book was set in Sabon
Printed and bound by Vicks Lithograph

Cover and interior design by Nick Panos
Cover photo by Denise Grant
Interior photographers: Denise Grant, Mark Gomes
Photos provided by Balazs Boxing on pages 26 and 29 courtesy of Scott McDermott
Photo on page 67 by Andy Dumas

McGraw-Hill books are available at special quantity discounts to use as premiums and
sales promotions, or for use in corporate training programs. For more information, please
write to the Director of Special Sales, Professional Publishing, McGraw-Hill, Two Penn
Plaza, New York, NY 10121-2298. Or contact your local bookstore.

In view of the complex, individual, and specific nature of health and fitness problems, this
book and the ideas, programs, procedures, and suggestions in it are not intended to
replace the advice of trained medical professionals. All matters regarding one's health
require medical supervision. A physician should be consulted prior to adopting any
program described in the book if the reader has any condition that may require diagnosis
or medical attention. The authors and publisher disclaim any liability arising directly or
indirectly from the use of this book.

This book is printed on acid-free paper.

Dedicated to our parents:

Eve and Cliff Dumas Sr.
Joyce and Joseph Lipton

CONTENTS

Foreword ix
Preface xi

CHAPTER 1
A Tradition of Sportsmanship 1
The History of Boxing: "The Sweet Science" 1
Amateur and Professional Boxing 2
Women in Boxing 4

CHAPTER 2
Fitness Boxing 7
If You Want to Look Like an Athlete . . . 7
The One-Two Punch Boxing Workout 7
Fitness Training Principles 8
Come Out Swinging 10

CHAPTER 3
Boxing Fundamentals 13
Boxing Basics 13
The Execution of a Punch 15
Shadow Boxing 19
Target Mitts 22

CHAPTER 4
Working the Bag 27
Protecting Your Hands 27
The Heavy Bag 29

The Speed Bag 33
The Double-End Striking Bag 36
Getting Your Kicks 37

CHAPTER 5
Learning the Ropes 41
Jumping Rope 41
Jumps and Combinations 43

CHAPTER 6
The Boxer's Workout 51
The Program 51
The Boxer's Workout 56
"Boxing Shorts" 57
The Champs Workout 58

CHAPTER 7
Cardio-Conditioning 61
Why and How a Boxer Does It 61
The Program 62
Equipment 62
Measuring Training Intensities 63
Cardio-Conditioning Workout 65
Flexibility and Stretching 66
Stretching Exercises 67
Some Standard Precautions 70

CHAPTER 8

Muscle Conditioning   **73**

The Program   73
Weight Equipment   75
The Exercises with Weights   76
The Medicine Ball   83
The Exercises with the Medicine Ball 84
Cool-Down Stretches   87

CHAPTER 9

What's Right About Boxing?   **89**

Looking for a Boxing Club   89

Sparring   90
What to Look for in a Trainer   91
Until the Last Bell   91

The One-Two Punch Boxing
Logbook   **93**

Charting Your Progress   93
Keep It Going   94
Boxing Shorts   94
The 12-Week Program Chart   95
The Champ's Workout   143

FOREWORD
THE ONE-TWO PUNCH

"Everything old becomes new again."

The raw training regimen of boxers was at one time for only the toughest of men. Hours of training time—practicing punches on the heavy bag and sparring in the ring—were spent to get ready for an event. Fitness boxing selects the best of this "old school" training and incorporates it with the latest scientific and technical information to give a unique blend of old and new training methods for an overall workout for both men and women. The information in this book will help you discover your ultimate fitness level and provide insight and inspiration to begin, continue with, and explore your personal fitness goals.

The One-Two Punch Boxing Workout takes you through a day-to-day workout schedule utilizing cross-training methods. The program is broken into three training sessions: fitness boxing training, cardio-conditioning, and muscle conditioning. Included is extensive information combined with pictures and diagrams describing all aspects of boxing training. The basics of throwing a punch are incorporated with tried-and-true methods of cardio- and muscle conditioning.

This program offers a safe and effective path for the beginner to learn the physical requirements of training like a boxer. The material is presented in a manner that will allow the newcomer the basis for developing a greater fitness level, as well as provide the seasoned physically active individual with a vigorous and challenging workout.

—*Dr. Donald A. Chu, Ph.D.*

Dr. Donald Chu has an extensive reputation in the areas of fitness and conditioning. As a past president of the NATA (National Athletic Trainer Association) and a current chairman of the Certification Commission of the NSCA (National Strength and Conditioning Association), Dr. Chu stays directly involved with the training of elite and professional athletes. He has worked with sports personnel such as the U.S. Olympic synchronized swim teams (1993–2000), track and field athletes, and professional tennis players. He has published six books, including Jumping into Plyometrics, *written articles for journals, and contributed chapters in many fitness and athletic training books.*

PREFACE
THE ONE TWO PUNCH

Andy's Inspiration

To be successful in a fitness program you need balance, consistency, and discipline. These things were passed on to me by my father, Clifford "Kippy" Dumas. His career as a professional boxer took him all over the United States and Canada. Originally from Windsor, Ontario, he fought most of his bouts in his hometown, as well as in Detroit and Chicago. He was onetime sparring partner to middleweight champion Jake LaMotta, also known as "the Raging Bull," and he fought on the undercard of the Sugar Ray Robinson–LaMotta title fight.

My father has the unusual distinction of being the first professional boxer of the modern era to win two bouts on the same night! After knocking out his scheduled opponent in the first round, he was invited back for an encore match and won a decision.

Many, many years later my dad's love of physical challenges continued, and at the age of 68 he entered an indoor rowing marathon. This was a 48-hour team event attempting to set a world record. His numbers (mileage) surpassed rowers half his age! To my family and me it was normal. It was, well, just Dad!

When I was in my early teens my dad purchased my first heavy bag. We hooked up a chain around

this great old tree that we had in the backyard. He showed me how to wrap my hands, put on my punching mitts, and said one word—*go!* Three rounds later I was completely exhausted. Pounding the heavy bag is a great source of tension release, a primal therapy of sorts. Not only does it burn serious calories and tone muscles, it also benefits the psyche. From that moment on I was hooked. To this day it's still the toughest workout I've ever done.

Ever wonder why boxers are in such great physical condition? The strong, taut, conditioned muscles, developed cardiovascular system, and superb agility and coordination have resulted from boxing's unique training workout. *Webster's Dictionary* defines a fad as "a short-lived fashion or craze." What I like to call "fitness boxing" is nothing short of a fitness frenzy that is sweeping North America. Fitness boxing offers something very unique. Unlike conventional workouts, boxing is not a means to an end, but is an end in itself. The punching bag offers not only fitness and strength, but, perhaps more important, sport. The agility, coordination, and spontaneous creativity required by the punching bag far exceed the mental stimulation achieved with treadmills or stair-climbing machines. And just knowing that you can pound the heavy bag for four or five rounds heightens your sense of security and personal confidence.

Boxing is more than just throwing punches; every part of the body is used. Bobbing and weaving while throwing combinations works the arms, legs, chest, back, abdominals, everything!

The One-Two Punch Boxing Workout incorporates training methods used by some of the world's best-conditioned athletes—professional boxers: shadow boxing, target mitts, speed-bag/heavy-bag work, skipping, muscle conditioning, and flexibility. We don't just scratch the surface of boxing in this workout!

Jamie's Inspiration

To be one's personal best involves many aspects of life. And each one intertwines with the others. The mind, the body, and the soul all work together, and

if they are cared for, coaxed, and massaged, each one of us can attain our very own personal best.

I believe in being physically active, to allow and to demand the muscles to reach, to contract, to relax, to extend, to push, and to pull. The muscles need to be lengthened and shortened, the heart wants to pump, and the whole human body awaits the many challenges and adaptations to physical activity.

Ballet was the first physical activity I was involved in, and this specific activity includes many of the challenges a human body would ever desire. The training demands focus, a developed fitness level, commitment, and passion. The muscles, the mind, and the body must move in specified synchronism to produce a wondrous visual outcome. Ballet requires the development of strong, lean muscle tissue, practice of each movement, repetition after repetition, and thousands of hours of rehearsal to obtain precise timing and extreme physical conditioning.

And there I am doing these wonderful petite tours across the floor, my head held high and my shoulders down and relaxed. Ahhhh! Take a look at those arms. Why are my hands in a tight fist? A quick jab and then a one-two punch combination and I hear my boxing coach yelling at me, "Just what are you trying to do?"

Boxing and ballet are so very different, and yet so similar. The commonality of practicing very sport-specific movements over and over, the focused attention, the delicacy of the reach, and the swift unobtrusive responsiveness that becomes instinctive set these two activities apart from others. Both disciplines keep you in touch with physical reality, kinesthetically aware of the appendages, muscles being worked until completely fatigued and resulting in exquisite bodies. Self-indulgence is not allowed. One's feelings cannot overwhelm the combinations or steps, and the movement must be allowed to speak for itself.

It is important to remember that a great performance is not possible without every element being met. However, some days not all the elements are in our control. The best you can do is to prepare yourself both physically and emotionally and work to your personal potential.

Take pleasure in the preparation of creating a strong, lean, healthy body. Take pleasure in the process of the training and the development of the musculature so every move you request from your body is strong and executed with perfection. Condition the heart so greater amounts of oxygen are more readily available for the working muscles, and take pleasure in the ability to create movement, whether it be slow and controlled or explosive and dynamic.

Special Thanks To:

Andrew Laudenslager, Peter Pecsvaradi, and Virginia Ellen Martinez of Balazs Boxing. Max Maxwell, Joey de Los Reyes of Martial Arts Fighting Academy, Dr. Donald Chu, John Kim of jumpUSA .com, Marty Winkler and Louis Garcia of Free-Style JumpRoping, Andrew Finnagen, Doug Ward of Ringside, Denise Grant, Marc Gomes, John Foulkes of Absolute Fitness, Peter Joseph, Janet Douris-Stringer, and especially Amanda and Meghan.

Cliff Dumas, Sr., Andy's Father, after a boxing match (on left)

CHAPTER ONE
A TRADITION OF SPORTSMANSHIP

The History of Boxing: "The Sweet Science"

The sport of boxing has always been a test of physical fitness and prowess. It started as a method of settling disputes, displaying a fighter's bravery, strength, courage, and brawn. Winning a fight placed the victor in high esteem in the community. All these characteristics remain in the sport to this day, but boxing has developed into a contest of skill, ability, talent, and commitment. Boxing had a primal beginning, with few rules, but it has matured into an intricate physical science of fighting.

In ancient Greece and Rome, boxing was a gruesome sport that combined wrestling and boxing and permitted all sorts of dubious behavior such as biting, kicking, and the use of iron studs placed on thongs worn on the hands. The matches were brutal and often ended with one of the fighters seriously injured or dead. It was only when boxing was brought into the Olympics in 668 B.C. by the Greeks, that protective gear, leather hand straps, and headgear were worn during the warm-up and practice sessions. These were the prototypes for today's equipment. The Greeks recognized and prized the *skill* of the sport even outside the

Olympic Games, and boxing took a giant step forward. However, during the reign of the Roman Empire, the gladiator style of fighting (using studs on the hand strap and fighting until death) became popular once again, and the appreciation of the skill behind boxing declined.

As history progressed, boxing continued to be a means of resolving disagreements in both England and Ireland. Matches in the early 1600s were held outdoors, wherever an audience would gather. There were few rules, and matches would continue until one of the opponents could not get up or, even worse, was pronounced dead. It was not until the later part of the 1600s that the practice of using only the fists became the acceptable method of boxing. The punches, though, could still be thrown anywhere on the body, and matches were not stopped.

In the 1700s, gambling was part of the entertainment at the boxing matches. Town champions would be supported by financial bets and, even though gambling was illegal, the aristocracy would sponsor fighters, allowing prizefighting. Boxing matches started to move indoors and might even be held in the parlors of wealthy homeowners. Boxing at that time became an elitist spectator event, creating a far different atmosphere from the old prize ring. King George I commissioned the first boxing ring in England to be built in Hyde Park, London, in 1723. Boxing was becoming a very popular pastime, and fencing clubs encouraged members to learn the skill of boxing. The foot movements and the offensive and defensive moves of fencing worked successfully in a boxing match. Guidelines for boxing matches evolved, and wrestling, biting, and eye gouging were eventually banned.

A British fighter named Jack Broughton saw his opponent die at the end of their fight, and he was determined that death and brutal injury should not occur in the sport of boxing. He developed the first set of official rules for boxing. These rules, known as the Broughton Rules of 1743, were accepted by fighters and fighting establishments and remained intact for nearly 100 years. The rules protected a fighter from being continually knocked down and gave a time limit of 30 seconds for him to get up off the ground and make it back to his side of the square for assistance from his second or cornerman. At this point, if he was badly injured the fight would be discontinued. Previously, if the fighter made it to his feet he could be knocked down again immediately, without any time for recovery or medical attention. The new rules also stated that the fighters could not hit or grab below the waist, pull on hair or breeches, or hit a person on the ground. If a fighter kneeled, he was considered to be down and fighting was stopped. Umpires, usually gentlemen selected from the spectators, were used to help make decisions on fair play. Broughton also promoted the use of boxing gloves (a lightweight muffler) during sparring practice and introduced the counterpunch and blocking moves. Boxing gloves or hand coverings were still not used in the matches, and even as late as the 1800s bare fists were allowed in North America. Rounds could go any length, and it was not unusual for bouts to go as long as four hours or more. The longest fight recorded lasted six hours and fifteen minutes, between James Kelly and Jack Smith in Australia in 1856. These fights were brutal and would not be allowed today.

It was not until 1867 and the development of the Queensbury Rules that a three-minute time limit was implemented for a round and a one-minute break was added between rounds. A bout could go to 45 rounds and last up to two hours and fifteen minutes. Eventually they were cut down to 20 rounds in North America, then 15 rounds. In the late 1980s all championship matches had a maximum of 12 rounds, and this is where the limit stands today. A bout in Europe is also 12 rounds.

The first U.S. state to legalize boxing was New York (1896) and then Nevada (1897). Previous to this, boxing was illegal, but it was tolerated at most establishments. In 1882 Madison Square Garden held its first boxing match even though it was not yet legal. It was not until the 20th century that boxing became well established and was legalized in a number of cities in North America and England. European countries did not accept legalized boxing until the 1920s and the 1930s, so most fighters traveled to the United States and Canada in the 19th century.

Weight classes were established in the 1850s, starting with three divisions: lightweight, middleweight, and heavyweight. The actual poundage fluctuated within each class, and this often caused disputes in championship bouts. In 1909 the National Sporting Club determined fixed poundage for eight classes, and in 1910 nine divisions were set. Today in professional boxing there are seventeen recognized weight divisions, and there are twelve weight divisions in amateur boxing.

Amateur and Professional Boxing

The thrill of being in command of the body; the hard physical work of withstanding the punches; the time practicing combinations, thinking of the feet, slipping and throwing a punch; and the feel of victory are common to both amateur and professional boxing. The conditioning, the functional techniques, and the finesse are alike. The governing bodies and rules are not alike, however, and even though the outcome is the same—with a winner and a loser—the fight in the ring is very different.

In England, the Amateur Boxing Association was established in 1880, and in the United States, the United States Amateur Boxing Federation (now USA Boxing) was established in 1888. Both were essential in developing the basis for clubs and in promoting safe competition for athletes of all ages and abilities.

In amateur boxing, the match is a contest of skill, not brute force, toughness, or aggressive power. Fundamentals are stressed, especially defensive moves. The foundation of amateur boxing is that boxing should be effective, fun, and safe, and strict rules are enforced to ensure protection. Amateur boxing requires commitment to learn and develop each day. Points are awarded by landing clean punches, without reference to the power or force behind the punch. A power punch that knocks an opponent down scores the same as a clean and effective left jab. An amateur boxer's intent is to outbox his or her opponent by landing many clean, effective punches and setting up defensive moves rather than knocking out the opponent. The boxer with the better technique and most effective punches will be the winner.

Amateur boxing is a highly regarded sport that does not focus on monetary gains. It is used as a vehicle to instruct sportsmanship and the values of physical conditioning and provides a positive path to release frustrations and energies as it builds self-confidence and character. The governing body arranges respected contests with bouts that are short, well supervised, and refereed; provides certified coaching programs; and acknowledges outstanding athletic achievements. Amateur boxing is at the heart of all boxing and is considered the purest form of boxing. It is the essence of the sport.

Amateur boxing takes more precautions than does professional boxing to ensure safety. The boxer must go through a physical examination before and after the competition. Protective equipment is mandatory for each competition, and the gloves and headgear are required to have exact combinations of a variety of shock-absorbing foams to reduce the impact of a blow. Rounds last for two to three minutes, and matches have three to four rounds. The referee makes safety the most important aspect of his or her job.

Numerous studies have documented amateur boxing's safety since the late 1990s, and the National Youth Sports Safety Foundation ranked amateur boxing safer than other amateur sports such as wrestling, football, baseball, soccer, and even bowling. More injuries were incurred in these sports than in amateur boxing.

The Olympic style of boxing is the basis of sportsmanship in amateur boxing, and many of the great male professionals had a taste of amateur boxing and Olympic glory: Muhammad Ali, Joe Frazier, George Foreman, Evander Holyfield, Sugar Ray Leonard, Lennox Lewis, and Oscar De La Hoya. Amateur boxing often gives the professional boxing arena its next contestants. It is a great training field to learn, practice, and develop into a professional boxer.

In professional boxing a skillful fighter is recognized and celebrated, but most fans want to see a fierce, brutal battle. No headgear is worn, and fewer safety precautions are enforced than in amateur boxing. The boxing gloves do not have the padding like amateur boxing gloves. The intent is to inflict pain and send your opponent to the floor as fast as possible.

There still is not a single set of rules that control professional boxing, so the rules change according to the governing body of the fight location. Most professional sports (like hockey, football, and soccer) have one set of rules no matter where they are played. In professional boxing some states' rules differ from other states'. For example, in one state there may be a three-knockdown rule and the fight will be stopped, while other states will allow the fight to continue.

Training and conditioning count for the majority of time that amateur and professional boxers spend on this sport. After working on fundamentals and developing physical conditioning, agility, and style, the boxer is ready to test his or her skills in the ring and prove his commitment to the sport.

Women in Boxing

The allure of boxing for women often starts with a commitment to get in the best physical condition possible. Boxing is a total physical fitness program. Muscle mass increases, fat percent decreases, and the body transforms into a strong, lean, powerful athletic structure. The training helps build agility, power, and endurance and has a crossover effect that benefits involvement in other sports. It builds self-confidence, self-discipline and self-discovery and is a great avenue to get rid of the frustrations of the day. Boxing training combines both physical and mental demands. A boxer has to develop an inner toughness and commitment to keep going. It is more the actual training than the physical contact that keeps many women involved in boxing. Boxing continually teaches something new, and it is not boring because there is so much variety in the training.

Boxing gives empowerment and a sense of equality to an individual. Boxing as a fitness workout is highly regarded, and making it through a workout provides a tremendous feeling of success. Women are attracted to this sport because of the skill and the thrill of an incredible physical and mental discipline. Every muscle is worked. Female boxers realize that size does not matter. It is the learning and the perfecting of technique that will result in victory, and they embrace this challenge in boxing.

Female boxing may revive the spectator sport of boxing. There is a new base of female viewers and a lot of interest in the unknown. Viewers know what to expect from the male professional fighters, but not from the females. Female fights move at a fast pace with two-minute rounds instead of three-minute rounds. There is a lot of action and many punches. As interest grows in the women's matches, more money is invested into the fights. Female fights get good coverage on high-priced TV fight nights, and all-female cards are part of the entertainment scene today. Many believe that women's boxing is a purer form of the sport. Women have the necessary focus, and with this commitment they develop solid boxing skills.

Female boxing became the phenomenon of the 1990s, but women really broke into boxing in the 1970s, perhaps influenced by the women's movement. There was resistance in the sport to allow women in the boxing ring, and most female fights were considered to be nothing more than a novelty act. It was believed that women simply were not built for boxing, but the pioneers trained hard, learned the skills, and opened up many opportunities for today's female boxers.

The first sanctioned women's fight in North America (by the Canadian Amateur Boxing Association) was an amateur fight, held in Sydney, Nova Scotia, Canada, in 1991, between Jenny Reid and Therese Robitaille. Canada became known as the place where women could participate in sanctioned fights, and it was not long before the USA Boxing Association also sanctioned female fights. This opened the door for a new era in boxing—women's boxing.

The female boxer is articulate, dedicated, disciplined, and highly motivated. These athletes are interested in learning the sport and realizing the highest level of boxing ability and expertise. There is a high level of skill, commitment, and focus. Female boxers fight with intensity.

A number of new women's professional boxing associations have started and often experience some of the same difficulties as the male associations. There are different rules for fights in different states. Some think that it may be best for women to stay involved only in the amateur ranks, where their skills will be acknowledged and where there is more control of the rules. But, as the ama-

teur base and clubs continue to grow, more women will have aspirations to experience the world of professional boxing.

Boxing training offers total physical conditioning, and numerous women start with this goal in mind. They attain great fitness attributes and learn the skills of boxing. They then step into the ring and feel the challenge of a lifetime. They use their newly developed strength and quickness, discover the intricacies of moving across the canvas, and throw punches round after round, hoping to be first to land the punch that will make them victorious.

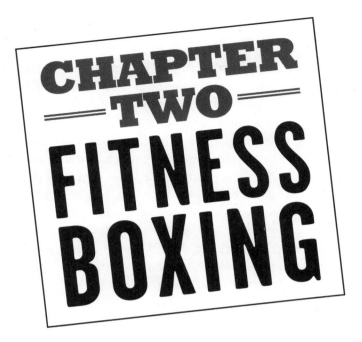

If You Want to Look Like an Athlete . . .

If you want to look like an athlete, you have to train like one, and boxers are some of the best-conditioned athletes in the world. Fitness boxing takes the best part of a boxer's workout and combines it with mainstream fitness. It is a unique workout that is not just a means to an end, but is an end in itself. Anyone wanting a new and different fitness training regimen will find fitness boxing challenging and rewarding.

An increasing number of people are searching for ways to improve their physique, and many have become plain bored with traditional exercises. Except for those training to become world-class athletes, most people begin activities like running, cycling, and swimming with sincere intentions to improve their health and fitness levels but quickly lose motivation. For the average person there is nothing inherently exciting about such exercises; they are simply routes toward the elusive hard bodies that we all crave, and without ironclad determination it is next to impossible to maintain inspiration for something that is monotonous. *The One-Two Punch Boxing Workout* gives you the inspiration and guidance to achieve the best-conditioned body obtainable. It takes the most beneficial parts of boxing training and combines them with mainstream fitness like running and weight lifting.

In this workout, many of the human body's physiological systems are worked, and a psychological sense of well-being is developed. The musculoskeletal system becomes stronger through the weight training (muscle conditioning) and boxing training workouts. The cardiorespiratory and vascular systems become more efficient during the running (cardio-conditioning) and boxing training workouts, and the central nervous system is trained to respond faster and more efficiently as it masters the intricacies of punching combinations and the execution of physical movements. Training like an athlete is hard work that leads to a wonderful sense of accomplishment and completeness.

The One-Two Punch Boxing Workout

The One-Two Punch Boxing Workout, one of the most demanding exercise routines available, involves all aspects of physical fitness, from brutal anaerobic workouts to the fine-tuning of precise execution of movement. The types of activities, the placement and the variety of the workouts, and the resting and rebuilding periods will not only encourage you to continue but will also enhance your total physical fitness level.

The workout starts off with the boxer's workout on Days 1 and 4, cardio-conditioning (roadwork) on Days 2 and 5, and muscle conditioning (weight lifting) on Days 3 and 6. Day 7 is a rest and rebuilding day. By working on all three sessions—the boxer's workout, cardio-conditioning, and muscle conditioning—you can attain an overall optimum fitness level.

Some of the benefits of the boxer's workout include improvements in the cardiorespiratory and vascular systems, increased muscular strength and improved agility, and quicker reaction times. This is accomplished by shadow boxing, hitting the heavy bag, practicing complicated punch combinations, heavy-bag speed sprints, and jumping rope. This portion of the workout keeps you in touch with the sport of boxing and develops a practical skill. Learning to coordinate muscle movements with the mind to produce a requested response is challenging and rewarding.

During the cardio-conditioning session, long and short runs, sprints, and cardio equipment are utilized according to the needs and likes of the individual. It is important to build a strong stamina base, working the heart muscle to respond to higher workload demands. This base will assist in future improvements in all areas of physical fitness.

The muscle-conditioning session develops muscular strength and muscular endurance using a variety of equipment—both free weights and machines. Training with the medicine ball offers a challenge to the musculature and develops balance, coordination, and a strong body core.

The One-Two Punch Boxing Workout challenges the physiological systems by cross training, reducing the chance of overtraining and possible injury at any one site. The program changes from day to day, preventing boredom and ensuring positive anticipation for the next workout. The body is able to respond correctly and skillfully to the training demands because of the program design and the inclusion of cross-training methods.

Remember, training in all three areas will create a positive cross-training effect. Working on just one of the training sessions, though, without the others, does not promote the same degree of physical change nor allow the body to develop into the best physical shape that can be attained. If you had to choose just one training session, however, the boxer's workout should be your choice. Boxing training involves muscular strength, endurance, and aerobic and anaerobic conditioning; it also improves agility, response time, balance, power, and finesse.

The One-Two Punch Boxing Workout is designed for a variety of fitness abilities. Some of the principles of fitness training—like adapting, overloading, cross training, interval training, and base fitness level—are reviewed.

Fitness Training Principles
Adaptation

The body meets the challenges placed on it from external sources and quickly learns the most efficient route to produce a movement. The electrical signals from the brain to the muscle tissue to produce a movement become very efficient and take the shortest and least complicated route to complete a task. The muscle responds with less hesitation and recruits fewer fibers to produce the movement. Therefore, fewer signals from the brain and fewer muscle fibers are required to produce a single movement.

When learning a specific technique for a sport, this adaptation is essential to improve the skill. Executing a movement over and over will teach the muscles to produce the desired outcome almost instantaneously, improving response and reaction time and efficiency. This allows for improved performance in the skill or the sport. But when this is applied to the training of the human body and its physiological systems, this adaptation will allow the body to find the easiest route. The result is an efficient system that will always work at the most efficient level. The training effect—the increase in musculature, cardiorespiratory volumes, and maximum exchanges of gases—will not improve unless more-than-expected demands are placed on the systems. The body learns quickly to adapt to the new demands placed on it, and these demands soon become old demands. The central nervous system knows how and when to execute a movement and then the movement becomes very efficient. Form follows function, and the body and muscles always try to adapt to the demands.

The Overload Principle

One method of keeping the physiological body from adapting is to frequently change the demands placed on it. Overloading a system (running longer, harder, faster; lifting more weight more times; or spending more time on an activity) will promote and maintain an improved fitness level. But it is important not to place such an overload that the supportive and connective tissues are at a risk of injury. A gradual increase and smaller changes are safe methods of placing new demands on your body.

Essentially, when an increased workload is placed on the body, the physiological systems are placed under stress. They will try to work to meet the new demands and in doing so may cause some damage at the basic cellular level. The systems will require time, rest, and nutrients to rebuild, and this is accommodated in a well-designed exercise program.

Cross Training

The workout design provides the cross training needed for you to easily attain success. Cross training, or alternating among two or more types of activities, not only reduces the risk of injuries from overtraining in one mode, but constantly surprises the body and forces it to adjust to diverse demands. The body performs activities, but not in the same manner as the previous workout, and the muscles and joints are given a rest and a chance to build and rebuild to an optimum fitness level. Training in the three different workout sessions—the boxer's workout, cardio-conditioning, and muscle conditioning—results in a significant reduction in adaptation to the exercise demands and overuse injuries. It also adds variety and fun to the program.

Interval Training

Interval training takes the workout to a higher intensity level for short periods of time interspersed throughout the training period. The overload is for a short enough time to not cause injury, but long enough to promote improved fitness levels. Workout intensities are increased gradually and for longer duration as the program progresses.

The One-Two Punch Boxing Workout utilizes interval training in the boxing training days, hitting the heavy bag and jumping rope, and in the later part of the cardio-conditioning days when running sprints are performed. The increased overload lasts from 20 seconds to a few minutes depending on the type of activity and your base fitness level.

Base Fitness Level

Everyone has a starting point from which to build a stronger and healthier body. Many contributing factors, such as heredity, age, and gender, will influence the ability of the body to respond to the demands placed on it.

Such factors as testosterone levels will influence the ability to develop muscle tissue and lift heavier weights. The cardiovascular and respiratory exchanges of oxygen and other relevant gases and lung and heart sizes will influence your running ability, fast- and slow-twitch muscle fiber percentages will influence agility, speed, and power. Limb length, muscle belly size, tendon insertion and length, and ligament striations will also influence your initial level of fitness, the fitness level you can attain, and the sports and performance levels that can be realized.

Each individual has abilities and capacities distinctive to him- or herself, and the goal of optimum fitness is to try to achieve the best physical condition in the areas of muscular strength and endurance, cardiovascular and respiratory endurance, flexibility, and body composition specific to the individual. The base fitness level, the starting point or current fitness level, will improve more quickly for someone starting at a lower level than for a more athletic individual. As one becomes more physically fit, it is more difficult to attain an even higher fitness level.

Come Out Swinging

Fitness is such an important part of life's journey because of the health and physical gains and the psychological, social, and self-worth benefits. To begin and continue along a new and different path in life (such as daily exercise) can be exciting and motivating, but more often it is difficult to get started and to persevere.

Most have tried exercise programs, have read about them, know what they should be doing, and may even have experienced the many benefits. But just knowing what you should be doing will not give you improvements in your fitness level. You cannot just think about it; you can improve only by doing the activity.

Some of the obstacles you may face when starting an exercise program are self-doubt, lack of confidence, nervousness, and self-condemnation. These obstacles are often based on negative past experiences, times when you have not been successful in performing an activity. If you are not in the habit of training or exercising, a positive attitude about exercising will not just occur sponta-

neously. The emotions readily available are only negative ones or none at all, and you do not have positive experiences to fall back on.

The mind habitually takes you back to unsuccessful times and inhibits you from performing. The lazy feeling or the feeling that you do not want to work out occurs because the thoughts and emotions of the unsuccessful times are the ones that pop into your head. To combat this, try to reflect on moments when you were at your best. Start building successful experiences and train your mind to go to these positive times, concentrating on how great it felt and the fact that you were successful.

If you become uneasy or nervous about performing an activity, reflect on positive experiences, stay calm, and enjoy the activity. Concentrate and focus on what you are doing and just experience the activity. Try not to give any rating to the performance, stay in the moment, and let go of the past and any failures. Remember, by starting and doing the activity you have already succeeded. Build on this feeling of accomplishment.

By paying attention to what you do, you will learn more than if you pay attention to what you have not done. This is one of the purposes of the logbook and record keeping. It helps you to stay on track, and when you look at all you have done, you can draw on the experiences to keep you motivated. When hitting the bag, feel the power in the arm, the contact with the bag, and the rebound off the bag. Try to become involved only in the activity, making the movements spontaneous and automatic. Think about the last run that felt great and then just start running again.

Exercising regularly gives you a sense of well-being. Missing a workout day will not feel right. On those days that you do not feel like exercising, try to discover why and then set aside that tiny voice that keeps telling you that you really do not want to expend the energy, that you are tired, or that you have more important things to do. Just start and if it does not feel right, then stop. Most times once you start exercising you will want to

continue, and even if you do stop, at least you have done more than if you never started.

Sticking to a workout program will carry over into other parts of your life and give you a feeling of empowerment. How we feel and perform is a function of how and what we think. The sense of well-being, relaxation, and joy carries over from the workout into the rest of your life. By making the process more important than the outcome, the outcome will result without stress and worry.

CHAPTER THREE BOXING FUNDAMENTALS

Boxing Basics

The Classic Boxing Stance

The boxing stance is the starting position for all boxing moves. If you are right-handed, start with the left shoulder and hip in a three-quarter stance to the target, with the dominant right hand being used for the powerful knockout punches. This is referred to as the classic or orthodox boxing stance and is used by the majority of boxers. If you are left-handed, the stance is called the southpaw stance. The left hand, being the dominant hand is used to land the power punches and the right shoulder and hip are angled closest to the target. The body is relaxed and balanced, which allows for a variety of movements to be effectively executed. Whether the moves are attacking (offensive) or protective (defensive), always try to come back to the classic boxing stance, as explained here.

The Legs and the Feet

Stand with the feet together, take the right foot to the side and place it hip-width away from the left foot. Next, step forward with the left foot. This is the starting foot position for a right-handed boxer. Left-handers will have to reverse the feet, left foot

Classic boxing stance

to the side, hip-width away from the right foot, and right foot forward. Equally center the body weight through the balls of the feet, and raise the back heel slightly. The position should feel balanced and allow easy movement from side to side or front to back. Slightly bend the knees so the legs can produce sufficient power to execute quick and strong movements. The legs must be able to react quickly, as well as act as shock absorbers. It is important, though to not bend the knees too much, as this will cause the body to be crouched over and produce awkward and sluggish movement across the floor.

The Body

Hold the torso in control, with the abdominals tight, and the shoulders slightly rounded forward and relaxed. Focus on the center of the body, and try to make all your movements start from this area. Align the front shoulder, hip, and foot, and have the body face the opponent on the angle, making the body less exposed.

The Arms

Hold the arms close to the sides of the body by the ribs, and bent at the elbow so that the hands are close to the face. By keeping the elbows and arms close to the body, you are better protecting the rib cage and solar plexus.

The Hands and Fists

Close the fingers loosely together to make a fist, with the thumb folding to the outside of the fingers. Turn the fist slightly inward. Hold the wrists straight and strong. Hold both fists close to the chin to protect the face. An orthodox boxer should hold the right fist slightly higher and very close to the chin while the left fist is just above the top of the left shoulder. (Southpaws should reverse the positions.) It is from this position that the punches are executed. Practice keeping the fists up whenever you are moving, unlike the great Muhammad Ali who danced with his arms held down at his sides. Ali had tremendous speed and agility to be able to move away from his opponent. Most do not.

The Head

Hold the head slightly down, with the chin tucked into the chest. Keep your eyes on your opponent, and keep that chin protected with the right fist and left shoulder (or left fist and right shoulder for southpaws).

Always try to set up in the classic boxing stance before throwing any punches or moving across the floor.

Footwork and Movement

The skill of moving across the canvas—of advancing, retreating, and moving left and right—has to be developed. The movement starts in the direction that you want to travel, and the rest follows. Advancing movements are initiated by stepping first with the forward foot then following with the back foot. Retreating movements are initiated by stepping first with the rear foot and then following with the front foot. To move left, move the left foot first and follow with the right; to move right, move the right foot first and follow with the left. Remember, never cross the feet or legs.

The boxer wants to move and shift his or her weight back and forth to set up an attack, as well as to avoid getting hit. Movement should be calculated and should help you achieve your goal. To move effectively, you must be relaxed and in control. If you find yourself not feeling in control, just take a break, find your center, and start again. You never want to be off balance. When shadow boxing or hitting the heavy bag, try to move around and imitate attacking and defensive movements. Remember that when you are actually executing that punch, the feet stay still, otherwise you will be off balance when contact occurs, and you will not be able to dodge a counterpunch.

In order to evade punches, you can retreat (move backward) or learn to slip the punches. Keep the torso tight and the feet on the floor, and move the body side to side away from the direction of the punch. Use the legs to lower the body into a crouched position to slip under the punch. Always

Slip to the right. When avoiding punches, don't overslip.

Slip to the left. Maintain balance and keep your eyes on your opponent.

remember to keep the fists up by the chin, the elbows close to the body, and the eyes on the target. Keep thinking about your next move.

Practice feints and slips mixed into the punch combinations. To feint, start to throw a punch, hold back, and then execute the punch. Set up right-handed punches with a left feint and left-handed punches with a right feint. To set up head punches, feint punches to the body and vice versa. The opponent expects one punch and is surprised by another.

The power for floor movement, slips, and feints comes from leg strength and the ability to push off the balls of the feet. Medicine ball–training and the

muscle-conditioning program will assist in the development of leg strength, increase the ability to push off the balls of the feet, and improve agility to return to a balanced position.

The Execution of a Punch

During the execution of a punch, the body is firm but relaxed. The legs push up, the trunk rotates, and the punching arm unwinds into an explosive, powerful punch. This synchronization among the leg, body, and arm movements develops from precise adaptation of the muscle fibers and the continuous execution of the jab, straight right, hook, and uppercut. The arm extends after the hips and shoulders move through the midline axis. Punching nonstop to the target, the arm travels along the same line away from the body and back toward the body.

A lot of technique is required to perform a single punch, and repetition after repetition is necessary to develop this skill. Attitude and focus also play a large part in training sessions. The mind must concentrate on every muscle fiber responding exactly in simultaneous movements. Punching imagery assists in feeling the punch, producing a stronger, better-executed movement. And to put together a number of single punches (punch combinations), quick thinking, explosive power, overall elite physical conditioning, and hours and hours of training are required.

The Left Jab

As the most frequently thrown punch, the main purpose of the jab is to keep your opponent off guard and at a safe distance and to set yourself up to throw a series of punches. It allows you to move your opponent backward, partially obscuring his vision. It is thrown with speed, accuracy, and frequency. Approximately 60 percent of all punches thrown in a match are jabs.

The jab is thrown in a straight line toward the opponent's chin, with the arm closest to the opponent. If standing in a normal orthodox stance, it is the left arm that snaps away from the body with a slight pivot at the left hip area and shoulder. Extending this arm fully, but not hyperextending it or "locking it out," punch the target rotating the forearm the last third of the distance. It is important to not pull the punch or stop the movement as the target is hit. If this is occurring, it is sometimes beneficial to visualize jabbing *through* the target. Keep the knuckles faceup and the palm down. Keep the whole body behind the punch, and push

Left jab

off the ball of the back foot while the front foot slides forward slightly. This all occurs just before the punch makes contact.

Keep the right fist close to the chin protecting it. Hold the elbow close to the sides of the body, protecting the ribs and body. After impact, bring the left arm back to the classic stance as quickly as possible, along the same line of delivery. Execute the delivery and retraction of the arm smoothly, allowing the body to remain balanced.

Vary the speed of the jab. Change the height of execution and perhaps lower it to make the opponent drop his hands. In doing so, you set up the target for counterpunches, like the straight right.

When working on the heavy bag, practice specific combinations with just the left arm. Try to execute two jabs back-to-back. Keep the first jab fast and light, then retract quickly, slide the foot forward, and add the second jab. Or jab to the body and then jab to the chin. Remember to execute from a centered, well-balanced position.

The Straight Right

The power of the straight right is produced from the simultaneous rotation of the hip and shoulder and the pushing or driving off the ball of the rear foot while stepping forward with the front foot. This punch takes more energy and time to execute than the jab. The body pushes off balance more easily, so it is important to tighten the abdominal muscles to maintain a strong center of balance and proper alignment. The body and head are left open to counterpunches, and therefore, you must try to return to the protective, balanced boxing stance as quickly as possible.

Starting in the classic boxing stance, rotate the right hip and shoulder forward and counterclockwise, and extend the right arm straight away from the body. Rotate the fist the last third of the punch with the thumb going from being on top to facing the midline of the body. Be careful not to wind up, lifting the rear elbow and executing the punch in a circular motion. This will indicate to the opponent that a punch is coming (called "telegraphing" the punch), and he or she will either counterpunch with an inside punch or move out of the way of your punch. At the time of impact of the straight right, the right shoulder is closer to the opponent than the left shoulder because of the strong torsion of the shoulders and body. Finish the punch with the hips square to the target, chin down, and eyes on the target. Always keep the left fist up to protect the chin.

The right cross is somewhat similar to the straight right, but the right cross has a slight arc as the punch is being thrown across the midline of the body. This occurs because of the slipping, side-to-

Straight right

side movement of the body while the punch is being thrown.

Practice some combinations on the heavy bag like the old one-two punch—a left jab followed by a straight right. Or, try a double jab and then a straight right to the target. (Throw two fast left jabs, sliding the foot forward to stay in range, and then a fast straight right.)

The Left Hook

The left hook is a punch that often catches the opponent unaware. This inside, tight punch must be executed at close range outside of your opponent's range of vision. It is because of the surprise element of the punch that it is not often blocked or countered successfully. The punch is generally effective after a straight right has moved the opponent backward. It can also be used as a counterpunch after slipping from a straight right. The power of this punch comes from the force of the rotation of the body that is transferred through the hooking arm, and not from just the force of the arm itself.

Starting in the classic boxing stance, hold the torso very tight and center the body weight through the rear leg. With the knees slightly bent, transfer the weight of the body to the left (front) foot. Swivel the front foot inward on the ball of the foot as you start to rotate the hips and shoulders. Pivot the entire upper body, and lift the left arm away from the body causing the inside of the arm to become parallel to the floor. Keep the elbow at a 90-degree angle. The fist should have the thumb pointing up and the knuckles facing toward the midline of the body. The force that is created through this punch is significant and is very effective, especially when it is a surprise. Finish with the elbow returning close to the body, fists by the chin and in the classic boxing stance.

To execute the hook effectively, throw it close to the opponent, so he or she cannot see it coming, but not too close, as your hooking arm will wrap around the opponent's neck. Remember to keep the chin tucked down behind the left shoulder and the right fist held up to block any counterpunches.

The left hook can be directed to the opponent's head or body. Bend the knees to move the body up and down, varying the location of where the hook is to land. Practice this on the heavy bag getting a feeling of staying close to the bag and keeping the arm at a 90-degree angle. Add a jab followed by a left hook. The jab will move the opponent back, and then you can move in with a hook to either the body or the head. Spend time developing a smooth hook off of the jab on the heavy bag. Also, practice slipping a right jab, then come back with

Left hook

a left hook to the body, or straighten up a little and hook to the head. Remember to stand close to the heavy bag when practicing the hook.

A hook off of the back foot is not an effective punch to throw. The head and body are left open to a strong counterpunch.

The Uppercut

The right uppercut is a very powerful and effective inside punch. The target must be at short- or medium-range punch distance. The uppercut is directed either high, toward the head under the chin, or low to the body, often in the solar plexus area. The uppercut can be thrown effectively with either the right hand or the left hand, with the right uppercut being slightly more powerful.

To throw a right uppercut, start in the classic boxing stance with the back (right) knee bent. Lower the right shoulder to drop the right side of the body in a semicrouch position. Remember to keep the left fist up by the chin to protect the head. Now as you rotate the hips forward, push off the ball of the back foot (the right foot), and punch the right fist up toward the target. The right side of the back and the right shoulder will follow through with the rotation of the hips. Finish with the hips squared to the front. Always keep the right arm close to the body and moving upward in a semicircle. For the most effective and powerful punch, keep the elbow bent at a right angle during the delivery and follow-through.

To throw the left uppercut from the classic boxing stance, start with hips squared off, left knee bent, and left shoulder lowered. Transfer the body weight to the ball of the left foot as you deliver the punch with a bent arm at a right angle and rotate the hips into the classic boxing stance.

Follow-up punches will depend on whether you throw a right or left uppercut, on whether it's high or low, and on the end hip position (squared front or angled). If the right uppercut were thrown high (under the chin), this would cause the opponent to straighten up. A left hook to the head is a great punch to complete this combination. A left uppercut to the head should be followed with a straight right. In both these combinations the body weight is shifted from side to side, and the second punch puts the body into a balanced position. Uppercuts to the body will cause the opponent's body to fall forward. Step away slightly and complete the combination with another uppercut to the head.

Remember when practicing the uppercut to stay close to the target. If the punch is thrown from the outside, the opponent will be able to easily detect

Uppercut

that the punch is coming and counter with an effective straight punch. An uppercut from the outside also loses some of its power because the arm is no longer bent at the elbow and cannot effectively transfer the total body's force in the upward movement.

Shadow Boxing

Floor movement and each of the punches have to be practiced over and over individually to perfect them. Once you become familiar and comfortable with the actions, then it is time to start to put combinations together.

A great way to perfect the punches is to practice in front of a mirror. Stand fairly close to the mirror. Start throwing punches slowly with the emphasis on proper execution and technique. Do not worry about speed or power. Save that for the heavy bag, double-end bag, or speed bag.

Check Your Classic Boxing Stance

- Body relaxed

- Feet in correct position, with left foot slightly forward and right foot hip-width away from and slightly behind the left

- Body weight equally centered through the balls of the feet, well balanced

- Knees slightly bent

- Torso held tight

- The front shoulder, hip, and foot aligned and the body angled to the target

- The arms held close to the sides of the body with the elbows in tight to the rib cage

- Fingers closed in a loose fist

- Fists turned slightly in and held close to the chin

Shadow boxing. Putting the punch combinations together.

First work on the straight punches: the jab and the straight right. You may want to change your stance to a southpaw (just reverse the classic boxing stance) and practice the punches. Ensure that the mechanics are correct and movement feels smooth. Then move on to the inside punches: the left hook and the uppercut. Add some movement to these punches, some slips and feints. Step forward as you throw a jab. Retreat back and throw some straight right punches. Start with simple combinations, like the one-two punch.

Mirror training will assist you in learning about executing the punches correctly and is a great way to warm up the body by increasing the blood flow to the muscles and the lubrication to the joints. If a move feels awkward, then break it down in front of the mirror. You will be able to see if you are off balance, if you are shifting your weight correctly, if the arms are held at the incorrect angle, or if the hands are held too high or too low. The time to correct a punch is in front of the mirror, not on the heavy bag. Always start slow with the basic punches, adding speed and combinations as you become more secure with the feel of movements. If a combination does not feel right, slow it down and break it into smaller combinations until the

Try to recognize the length of a round. In the One-Two Punch Boxing Workout, the three-minute round is used throughout, and you will learn to pace yourself. Try to work hard enough that you will feel slightly out of breath but ready and eager for more. Take the minute in between rounds to think about new combinations, both offensive and defensive. Also, think about what did not feel smooth, how your body weight is shifting, where hands were and what felt great.

Throwing Effective Combinations

The finish of one punch should set you up for the start of the next punch. If the first punch puts you off balance slightly, the next punch should put you back on balance. For example, a straight right will leave the body in the perfect starting position for a left hook. The completion of the left hook will bring the body back to the classic boxing stance and in balance for the next punch.

Double up on your punches. Throw two jabs or two hooks consecutively. This will throw the opponent off, because it will be unexpected after only single punches have been thrown. Be aware, though, that the time between the punches will be longer because you must go back to the starting position in order to execute the punch correctly. With practice, the in-between punch time will decrease as the body moves in and out of position quickly.

Try to vary the height of the punches. Not only will this give you a better overall workout, it will also keep the opponent on guard. Practice combinations throwing punches to the body area, then throw in a few higher-placed punches. Spend time keeping the punches aimed higher and then drop a few. Incorporate feints and slips, moving the body from side to side. Also, vary the speed of the punches. Do not be predictable! For example, throw three left jabs at three-quarter speed and then one really strong fast jab.

punches and movements flow from one to the other.

Now move away from the mirror, and start putting more movement and punches together. You should always have a purpose when you shadow box. Match the footwork with the punches, and always have a mental image of what you want to do. Keep it simple at first, then decide where you want to hit and what punch you want to throw. Try to find a rhythm you are comfortable with and move around. Shadow boxing is rehearsal for the heavy bag and not just a muscle warming or loosening exercise.

Think about the punches and learn which one is your most effective and which one is your preferred. Place your best or favorite punch at the end of a sequence, or feign the most effective punch and deliver a rapid combination of a different punch. Mix it up!

Classic Combinations

1. The one-two punch (a left jab followed by a straight right)

2. Left jab—straight right—left hook

3. Right uppercut—left hook

4. Left jab—left hook—straight right—left hook

5. Left jab—left hook to the body—left hook to the head—straight right

6. Left jab—left uppercut to the body—left hook to the chin

Practice these combinations in front of the mirror, then move out onto the floor and shadow box. Note how the end of one punch is the starting position of the one that follows. Add foot movement, advancing and retreating. Then take it to the heavy bag. (Refer to "Hitting the Heavy Bag" in Chapter 4.)

Target Mitts

If you get a chance to train with another person, a great way to improve your punching speed and accuracy is to use target mitts. Training with target mitts is the next best thing to actually sparring. The punches should be light, and the technical execution of the punch should be of prime importance. The puncher learns to react quickly and effectively. Improving the strength and power behind a punch should be done on the heavy bag.

If you have never used target mitts before, start with only one target mitt and have the person doing the punching throw straight basic punches. With all the punches directed at one target mitt, there is a reduced risk of confusion about where to throw the punches and less chance of injury.

The person holding the target mitt is known as the "catcher," and the person throwing the punches is known as the "puncher." The catcher is the one in control and tells the puncher what combinations to throw. The target mitt is held one-and-a-half feet to two feet away from the body, arms slightly bent at the elbow in a semitense position. The legs and feet should be in a classic boxing stance to add stability to receive the punches, and the body core (torso) should be kept tight and strong. The puncher must always be kept in view. The second hand can be placed behind the hand holding the target mitt to give additional support to receive the punch. When the puncher hits the mitt, the catcher should allow the arms to absorb the punch by bending slightly at the elbows.

The puncher should stand in front of the catcher, in a classic boxing stance ready to execute a punch. He or she should stay slightly more than a jab length away, always keep the eyes on the target, listen to the punches the catcher calls, and throw with the purpose of improving punching technique, accuracy, and speed. There should be little intent of power in the punches. The idea is to get the feel of throwing a punch.

When starting, the catcher should call for the basic straight punches and add combinations once the puncher is comfortable with accuracy and responding quickly. The catcher should remind the puncher that there should be no intent behind the punch and to keep at least a jab length away. Once you both become comfortable with the basic punches, add footwork and movement forward, backward, and from side to side.

Putting combinations together using both target mitts is as easy as 1-2-3. The catcher holds both mitts in front of the body and stands in the classic boxing stance. Again, the arms should be slightly

Target mitts

bent in a semitense position ready to receive the punches. Assuming the puncher is in an orthodox stance, all jabs (left hand) should be thrown at the catcher's left-hand target mitt. All straight rights are thrown at the catcher's right-hand target mitt. Left hooks should be thrown at the catchers left target mitt. The catcher must turn the mitt inward to receive this punch. Right uppercuts are thrown to the right target mitt. The catcher must turn the target mitt down to be able to catch this punch. Having the puncher throw across to the opposite target mitts helps to keep the punches straight in front of the body. It also helps to develop a slight rotation in the upper body to assist in improving the execution of the punches and strengthening of the torso.

Puncher delivers the left jab to the catcher's left target mitt.

Puncher delivers straight right to the catcher's right target mitt.

Catcher turns left mitt inward to receive the left hook.

Right uppercut

Left uppercut. Catcher turns the mitts down to receive the punches.

Sample Combinations

Try cueing the punches with the following number:

1 = Left jab

2 = Straight right

1, 2 = Left jab—right cross

3 = Left hook

1, 2, 3 = Left jab—right cross—left hook

4 = Right uppercut

Slipping. As the target mitt moves towards the puncher, the puncher moves into the crouch position.

The puncher moves under the target.

The catcher calls the numbers and gets the target mitts ready to receive the punches. The puncher learns to react quickly.

Advanced Target Mitt Moves— Slip Drills

The catcher simulates a left hook and moves an extended arm side to side over the head of the crouching puncher. The catcher should keep the arm movement at his or her own shoulder height, no lower, no higher. The puncher starts in the boxer's stance and bends down in a slight crouch as the mitt moves overhead. The puncher uses the legs to lower and raise the body and should keep his or her eyes on the target, moving out of the way of the mitt. Perform this exercise for 30 seconds and then go back to punch combinations. Slips are a great workout for the legs and for developing core body strength.

Keep looking at the target as you finish the slip.

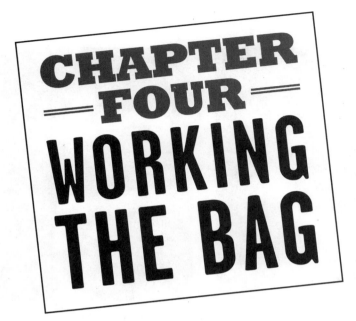

CHAPTER FOUR
WORKING THE BAG

Training on the bags (heavy bag, speed bag, and double-end bag) will teach you a lot about your technique, ability, and punching style, and there is this great spontaneous creativity involved in hitting the bag. It not only gives you immediate feedback; it is also the one and only time in the training program that you will feel the power, strength, and speed behind your punches. Directing the punches to the heavy bag can be a great release of tension and builds punching power and strength. Hitting the speed bag will teach you quickness and improve coordination. Punching the double-end striking bag will test and develop your agility and reaction time.

Before you put the gloves on and start the workout of your life, it is important to protect your hands with handwraps.

Protecting Your Hands
Handwraps

Reusable protective bandages are wrapped around the wrists, hands, and knuckles to give wrist support and prevent abrasions of the knuckles. The wrist and the hand become one strong unit, which is important when hitting the heavy bag. There are

a number of different techniques of hand wrapping, and each is ritualistic to the coach and boxer. It is important to wrap with an even tension and not too tight at any one place. The wrap should feel tight enough to give support, but not so tight that the circulation is impinged. Wrapping the same way each time will help you determine the right amount of tension.

Described here is a basic hand-wrapping technique that will give support to the wrists and protect the hands.

1. Place the loop of the wrap around the thumb, with the wrap falling to the front side of the wrist.

2. Wrap twice around the wrist and then once around the thumb.

3. Spread your fingers and wrap around the hand and knuckles four to five times. Keep the wrap flat, without any bulges, overlapping the side edges slightly to prevent spaces where the skin could extend through.

4. With the remainder (wraps come in a variety of lengths), continue to wrap

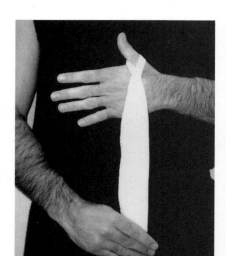

The loop of the wrap is place around the thumb.

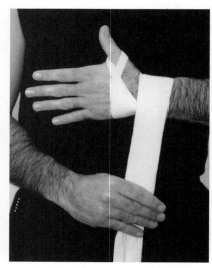

Wrap twice around the wrist.

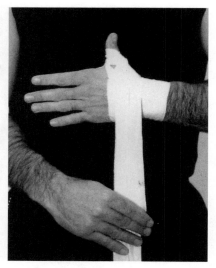

Wrap around the thumb.

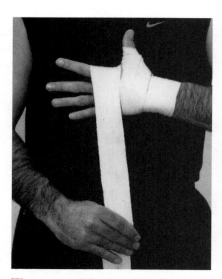

Wrap around the knuckles four or five times.

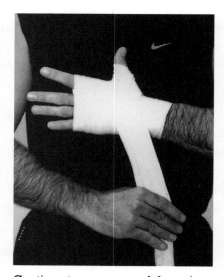

Continue to wrap around the wrist, hand, and knuckles.

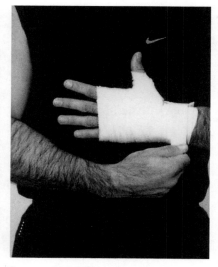

Secure with Velcro fasteners.

around the wrist, hand, and knuckles in a figure-eight pattern.

5. Leave enough handwrap to finish two to three times around the wrist, and secure with the Velcro fasteners or ties.

Whether you are putting on boxing gloves or striking mitts (bag gloves), you should wear wraps on the hands. They can be used on their own when working on the speed bag or when practicing light punching technique on the target mitts. Otherwise, either a boxing glove or a striking mitt covers them.

Boxing Gloves and Striking Mitts

Boxing gloves come in sizes from 8 ounces to 20 ounces. Generally, during boxing matches

10-ounce gloves are worn. The heavier gloves are worn in workout sessions to train the arm and upper-back muscles for endurance and power and during sparring because of the additional padding. The striking mitts have less padding than the boxing gloves and are worn only during training sessions on the double-end bag, speed bag, and target mitts. The boxing gloves are worn when training on the heavy bag to give additional protection to the hands and the wrists. There should be substantial padding in the gloves so the knuckles are protected upon impact on the bag. The gloves should have enough room inside to allow for circulation in the hand, but they should not be so roomy that the hand moves around. The palms of the gloves are slightly padded and molded to ensure secure fit around the hand. The exterior of the gloves is made of leather and the interior of foam padding. A thumb strap is usually found on boxing gloves today, especially those worn in the ring. This protects the thumb from being sprained or dislocated and protects the opponent from getting a thumb in the eye. Striking mitts usually have elastic or Velcro fasteners at the wrist and can be pulled on and off easily. Boxing gloves have elastic, Velcro, or laces to fasten them at the wrist area. Velcro fasteners at the wrist give great support and make it easy to put on and take off the gloves. It is most important that the gloves feel comfortable and have sufficient padding to absorb the shock of the impact from the punch on the heavy bag.

The Heavy Bag
Types of Heavy Bags

There are a variety of materials, sizes, and weights of heavy bags specific to training needs and individual requirements. The materials used on the bags range from leather, the most durable and expensive, to canvas, which is the least expensive and has that traditional look. The canvas bag has a rough texture and is hard on your gloves. A midpriced material replacing traditional canvas is

The Balazs Universal Boxing Stand (UBS₄)

a vinyl-coated canvas. The vinyl-coated canvas surface cleans easily, costs less than leather, and has great durability. Hanging bags weigh from 50 pounds to 150 pounds. The heavier ones move less but are also less forgiving and more jarring when they are hit. Floor bags can weigh up to 400 pounds, with most weighing between 150 and 250 pounds. The additional weight is needed to keep the bag from moving when being punched. They are fairly portable, are easily placed in an exercise area, and can be purchased at most sporting-goods stores.

There is, however, nothing like training on a hanging bag, being able to have the movement and hitting with all your power. Balazs Boxing has designed a freestanding heavy-bag holder that not only supports the heavy bag but also has a platform for the speed bag and a location for a double-end striking bag. The UBS₄ (Universal Boxing

Stand) is strong and very versatile, lending itself to effective and creative workouts. It is easily put together and has a variety of configurations to best suit different locations and individual needs.

The bag that meets your needs will depend on your experience, weight, height, and punching strength. Balazs suggests that a 70-pound hanging bag is a good starting size for the average person. Some of the bags are water filled, providing a surface that is softer and will reduce the jarring kick back of the punch. Other bags are connected on both ends, known as a double-end heavy bag, and are great for beginners and for practicing kicks.

Hitting the Heavy Bag

The best part of working out on the heavy bag is that it can be a different workout each and every time, with an endless number of punch combinations being executed. It is an exceptional workout that can place extreme demands on the musculature, cardiovascular, and respiratory systems. It is creative, fun, and a great way to release tension and stress, giving you a feeling of accomplishment and competence. Use your imagination—making up combinations, slipping, circling the bag—and the result will be punches with speed and power. Be creative. Think about it. Put passion into your punches and have the fight of your life.

The first thing you must do is wrap your hands and put on the gloves. The gloves should feel comfortable and your hands should fit deep into them. When the glove makes contact with the bag, the fist should be tight, the wrist straight, and the front of the glove touching the bag. Find your reach (the punching distance that you should be away from the bag) for a straight punch by positioning yourself with a fully extended arm at the moment of contact. Hooks and uppercuts require that you stand closer to the bag in order to make contact and hit to one side.

For the straight punches, try to hit in the center of the bag. This will help prevent it from spinning. After your first strike, hit the bag again as it is returning back toward you. If you try to hit the bag when it is moving away from you, and you do make contact, it may swing and swivel even more and become impossible to hit. And, if you miss the bag completely there is a good chance that your arm will overextend at the elbow and you may become injured. When the bag starts to spin, then either you are not hitting in the center of the bag or you are pushing your punch. The punch should snap out, hit the center of the bag, and then pull back and recover immediately. Do not leave your glove on the bag, but snap back.

Practice each of the punches until they are mechanically correct and then add more speed and power. If you are a beginner, work on a single technique for every round and then mix it up once the movements are second nature. Work the bag like you are in the ring, moving around and incorporating the back-and-forth movement of the bag into your workout. When the bag is moving away, step in closer and execute a punch, then back away. Stay light on the feet, including side-to-side movement of the feet and body. Slipping and ducking will help to develop torso strength and teach you about centering the body weight. Pivot the feet when you hit the bag to maintain the balance of the body and to provide a stance from which a maximum power punch can be executed. Never stand flat-footed, but stay on the balls of the feet, ready for movement. To add some power to the jab, tighten the abdominals (core muscles) and twist the body as the punch is being delivered—a good stiff jab.

Develop an action plan for working the bag, and have a mental image of your combinations. Experience the workout. It is not a competition to see who can throw the most punches, but a finely orchestrated plan of what punches to throw and how and when to throw them. Put power behind the punches and then snap them at the end. Feel the workout, enjoy it, and develop it.

The following few steps will assist you in starting to train on the bag. Once you master the basics, move more on the floor around the bag, attack and retreat, and develop and perfect your own combi-

Boxing stance in front of the heavy bag

Left jab. Establish your punching range.

nations. Remember, use the swinging motion of the bag to your advantage. If the bag is moving away from you, use your feet to get into position to reach the bag. If the bag is swinging toward you, back up, maintaining the same punching distance from the bag.

Step 1 Take your boxing stance in front of the bag, always returning to it throughout your workout.

Step 2 Determine your reach or your punching distance. Execute a jab. As you extend the arm, the glove should be in tight contact with the bag. Repeat a few times to get comfortable.

Step 3 Focus and hit in the center of the bag. Watch as the bag moves away and hit it directly and quickly as it returns to you. Mix up the straight punches, a few jabs, and then a straight right.

Step 4 Next, add movement and more power. Step into the punches and step out. Move the punching hand forward as the front foot moves forward. The hand returns to the shoulder as the foot returns to its original spot.

Step 5 Now have a plan and mix it up a bit. Move around, slip, and throw a few jabs to determine your reach and target area. Move in closer to the bag and throw hooks and uppercuts.

Sample Combinations

The One-Two Punch Throw a left jab followed by a straight right in rapid succession. Slip and move and repeat. (NOTE: Almost every punch combination should start with the left jab.)

Straight right on the bag

Left hook on the bag

One-Two Hook Step into the bag as you launch your left jab, followed by a straight right. You should now be in position to throw a short left hook to finish the combination. Step away and circle the bag as you plan your next sequence of punches.

Jab to the Body—Jab to the Head Step toward the bag and launch a quick left jab to the body, and immediately follow with a jab to the head. Move around and circle the bag. You can add a straight right onto this combination: jab to the body; jab to the head; throw a quick, straight right; move away; and repeat.

Left Jab—Left Hook As you move around the bag, step in and throw a quick left jab followed immediately by a left hook. Move around and repeat. (To throw the hook effectively, bring your arm back only halfway after you throw the jab.)

One-Two—Hook—Hook Throw a quick one-two to the body, then throw a left hook to the body followed by a left hook to the head (a double left hook). Repeat.

Advanced Six-Punch Combination Throw two left jabs (double jab), a straight right, a left hook to the body, and a straight right. Finish with a left jab as you back away from the bag. Move around and repeat.

It is important to not just start hitting the bag without a plan. You will exhaust yourself, risk the chance of injury, and have the feeling of defeat. As with any new activity, learn the technique and build up your stamina to be able to continue the activity. Remember that you are working toward three-minute rounds; you will have to learn to pace your workouts and mix up punches and foot movement.

Right hook on the bag

Right uppercut to the body

NOTE: For a balanced fitness workout, practice the punches on both the right side and the left (orthodox *and* southpaw stance).

The Speed Bag

A speed bag is a small punching bag that is suspended below a platform (horizontal backboard) on a swivel hook allowing for free rotational movement. It can be mounted on the wall or from a stand. The bags come in various sizes with the exterior made of stitched leather and the inside filled with a rubber air bladder. The largest speed bags are around 14 inches long and will move slower than the smaller-sized speed bags. The smaller bags—around 8 inches—move faster and rebound quickly, making them the most difficult to hit. Working the speed bag develops eye-hand coordination and improves reaction time, rhythm, and

Speed bag

upper-body endurance. It initially may be very frustrating, but ultimately it is fun and worthwhile.

Face the bag straight on.

Make contact with the knuckles.

Hitting the Speed Bag

When watching a boxer hit a speed bag, one wonders, How can you make contact with something moving that fast? And if you listen, it is the sound of the rhythm of the bag hitting the backboard that inspires one hand moving over the other to make contact with the bag. There are actually three sounds on the backboard that you hear. Stand facing the bag, strike the bag, and the bag will move directly away from you and make contact with the platform (sound #1). The bag will rebound toward you and hit the front of the platform (sound #2). The bag then returns to hit the back of the platform (sound #3), and you must get ready—as the bag rebounds forward it is your turn to strike it once again. The rhythm is punch-1-2-3. You hit the bag; the bag hits the platform back, front, and back.

The surface of your knuckles making contact with the bag and how hard you hit it will influence your ability to keep the bag under control and in the punch-1-2-3 rhythm. Start with one hand,

using a medium force until you have mastered the rhythm; then add the speed and power, alternating the hands. Do not wear boxing gloves. Use speed-bag striking mitts if your hands are sensitive; otherwise, handwraps give the basic protection required.

Step 1 Face the speed bag so it is square with the body; bring both fists up and in front of the face. This is the one time you do not have to be in the boxing stance. The bottom of the bag should be one to two inches above chin level for the larger bags and eye level for the smaller bags. If the bag is wall mounted, you may want to find a large bench to stand on, and if it is mounted on a stand like the UBS₄, then slide the platform to the appropriate height.

Step 2 Strike the bag in the center near the bottom edge, making sure the knuckles land flush against the leather. (There is a style of hitting the speed bag with the sides of your hands, but we prefer to keep consistency in the execution of the punches

Follow through with your punch.

Repeat striking the bag in a 1-2-3 rhythm.

and make contact with the knuckles.) Visualize hitting through the bag, and then bring the fist back to the starting position.

Step 3 Repeat striking the bag with the punch-1-2-3 rhythm, keeping both hands up by the face. Work with one fist, then the other, taking the arm through a circular motion. As you punch faster, tighten up the circular range of motion that the arm goes through.

Step 4 Go slow at first, and if the bag is moving too fast, try a larger-sized bag or let some air out of the bladder to slow it down. The bag will appear to have a mind of its own and may either move in circles or not respond to your strike. It's all a matter of timing. If you make contact too soon, you will jam the movement of the bag; if contact is made too late, your fist will strike the underside of the bag and cause a clumsy rhythm.

Step 5 Strike the speed bag four times with your right fist and then four times with your left fist,

eventually taking it to two strikes with each fist. Once you have mastered the doubles, try making single strikes. This is called a two-handed rhythm and requires that one fist is brought up behind and over the top of the other. For example, as you strike the speed bag with your left fist, bring the right fist up behind and over the top of the left fist and then strike the bag with the right fist. Repeat, keeping the semicircular movement short and fast.

Sample Combinations

1. Strike with only the left fist, keeping the right stationary.

2. Repeat, but use only the right fist.

3. Remember to hold the nonstriking fist up by the chin.

4. Decrease the number of strikes with each fist alternating from side to side.

5. As you want to decrease the number of strikes between fists, keep the nonstriking fist circling up behind the striking fist and then over, ready to make a strike on the speed bag.

The Double-End Striking Bag

There is no need for a sparring partner when you have a double-end striking bag. The double-end striking bag comes in a number of sizes, much like the speed bag, and has an air-filled bladder. Generally made out of leather, it can also be constructed with vinyl-coated canvas. A rope suspends the bag on the top, and an elastic shock cord holds the bottom to give an unforgiving rebound action when it is hit. Because the surface is so much smaller than that of the heavy bag, the double-end striking bag develops eye-hand coordination. Power is not the purpose behind these punches; rather, improving coordination, reactions, timing, and agility is the intention.

There is an entirely different rhythm to hitting the double-end bag than any other bags. Heavy bags don't punch back; double-end bags do! You learn to bob and weave, slip and duck, keep your hands up, and move your head. When you strike the double-end bag, it will move quickly away, then rebound back right at you.

You can wear either your boxing gloves, striking mitts, or handwraps when hitting the double-end striking bag. Start with the gloves and work toward using just handwraps or striking mitts.

Step 1 Address the bag in your boxing stance; keep your hands up, and get ready to move. Stay light on your feet, the weight centered more toward the front of the feet.

Step 2 Strike the bag and slip out of the way of the rebound. Work on technique, not power. Try

Double-end striking bag

to strike in the center of the bag at first, making the bag move directly back and straight at you. Move out of the way and then strike the bag again. Practice your slips, add footwork, move in and out, circle the bag, and mix up the punches.

Sample Combinations

Left Jab Slip to the right, throw a quick one-two, and slip to the left.

Double Jabs Slip and move out, then move in for a double jab and then a straight right.

NOTE: Training on the double-end striking bag will improve your coordination, agility, and punch speed. Save the power and the strength for the heavy bag.

Strike the bag in the center.

Bring your hands back, prepare to slip.

Slip the rebound and quickly return to the boxing stance.

Getting Your Kicks

Adding kicks to your workout provides another element to your fitness program. Kicking not only works the leg muscles effectively but also improves the torso strength that must be held tight in order to execute the kick properly. Because the legs have such a large proportion of muscle tissue, a lot of energy is required to execute a kick, which in turn burns a lot of calories. There are many outstanding and different types of kicks that you will see in the movies that look impressive and very complicated. Be aware, though, many of these kicks can be more dangerous to yourself than to your opponent and generally have a low rate of successful contacts. It is best to concentrate and learn three basic kicks: the front kick, the side kick, and the roundhouse kick. These kicks are safer and are the basis for any combination. They are also more effective than other kicks.

Starting in a classic boxing stance, the first movement in any kick is the drawing of the knee up to the body in preparation for striking (called the "chamber"). Hold the torso tight and the body weight balanced on the supporting leg. The supporting knee should be slightly bent with the weight through the center of the foot. Next, extend the lower portion of the kicking leg with force toward the target. Make contact with the foot, and then return the leg toward the body to the chamber position. Lower the leg to the floor. The lifting of the knee, the forceful extension of the lower portion of the kicking leg, and the recoiling back to the starting position are what make kicking challenging. The leg must travel through a large range of motion in a short period of time. Once you feel balanced and comfortable with the kicks, try some on the heavy bag. Remember to keep the hands up by the chin—in the classic boxing stance—and your eyes on the target while you are executing the kicks.

Front Kick (Right Foot)

Start in the classic boxing stance, with the left foot forward for right-handers. Shift the body's weight forward to the left foot while lifting the right knee

All kicks start from this position.

Front kick. Lift your right knee as you prepare to launch the front kick.

Extend your leg and make contact with the ball of the foot.

up in front of the body (the chamber), with the right thigh about waist level. Extend the right leg and push the foot forward and away from the body. Strike the target with the ball of the foot, keeping the toes curled back. When starting out, keep the kicks low, gradually lifting them higher until you reach chest height. Remember to keep the body weight slightly forward as you initiate the front kick. These kicks will increase balance, agility, and leg strength.

Short Side Kick (Left Foot)

Start in the classic boxing stance, with the left foot forward. Rotate the shoulders and the chest a few inches to the right, with a slight lean backward. Center the body weight over the rear (right) foot. At the same time, lift the left knee up to waist level. Extend the left leg straight out toward the side, with the toe pointing to the right. Make contact with the bottom of the left foot, primarily with the heel. The short side kick is slightly more difficult to master and is a greater challenge on the body.

Roundhouse Kick (Right Foot)

Start in the classic boxing stance, with the left foot forward. Pivot on the left foot, twisting the hips to the left while raising the right knee to around waist level. Extend the right leg in a semicircular movement forward toward the target. Contact the target with the top of the foot, where the shoelaces cross.

Practice all the kicks individually in front of a mirror, continually checking your body stance to ensure it is balanced and in the correct position to execute the different kicks. Then take them to the bag using a kicking bag or a heavy bag. Kicking bags are often softer, do not swing as much, and are more forgiving than heavy bags because of the double-end construction and stuffing material (often water). Also, be aware that there will be a rebound from the bag. Kicks that flow and feel smooth in the air may feel awkward and sloppy when first done on the bag.

Step 1 Take your boxing stance for the kick you want to execute. Bring the leg into the chamber position and extend the leg toward the bag to find

Starting kick position

Side kick. Lean slightly on an angle to the side.

Extend your leg towards the bag and make contact with the bottom of the foot.

Starting kick position

Roundhouse kick. Pivot to the left side and raise your right knee.

Extend your leg and make contact with the top of the foot.

your kicking reach. Return to the starting position and add more power to the extension of the leg.

Step 2 Practice one kick at a time on each leg until it becomes instinctive.

Step 3 Add movement away and toward the bag between the kicks. Add some punches to the kicks.

Sample Combinations

Front Kicks Execute a front kick, and then step in with a one-two punch combination.

Side Kicks Start in the boxing stance, throw a double jab followed by a straight right, slip back, and side kick with the left leg.

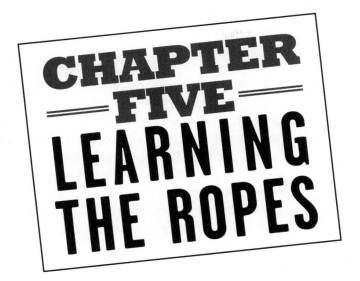

Jumping Rope

High school gym teachers loved jump ropes for two reasons. They were cheap and cruel! (The ropes, that is, not the teachers.) Even the top high school athletes would barely survive a fast 15-minute set of rope jumping. It can be more physically demanding than cycling (indoors or outdoors) and running. It improves cardiovascular fitness, develops endurance musculature, and improves agility, balance, and timing.

Professional boxers jump rope as part of their fitness training. The greatest boxer of all time, Muhammad Ali, would dazzle his opponents with his fancy footwork, then throw a barrage of lightning-fast punches. Ali would dance around the ring and shuffle, rapidly alternating his feet front and back. If you ever had the opportunity to watch him shuffling his feet while jumping rope, keeping time, and moving smoothly, you understand how he was so successful when he danced across the canvas during a fight.

Jumping rope requires a level of discipline not found in other aerobic activities. It is important to stay focused and in control, all the while concentrating on the feet, balance, and timing. It will take some time and commitment to master the basic jumps, but once this is accomplished, a wide variety of combinations can be performed. This not only makes the workout fun, it also challenges a large variety of muscles. It works the glutei, quadriceps, calves, and hamstrings. In the upper body, the back and chest muscles, deltoids, forearms, biceps, and triceps are recruited to produce the movement of rotating and stabilizing the rope. To maintain proper body alignment and a correct center of gravity, the abdominal muscles are recruited to contract and hold the body position. Jumping rope challenges the cardiovascular system and improves coordination, which in turn helps to develop agility, timing, power, and speed.

It's a great total-body workout to improve overall aerobic conditioning. Or, as Marty Winkler of FreeStyle JumpRoping states, "If your goal is to burn calories and fat and lose weight, no other exercise holds a candle to jumping rope. Because it requires the use of the upper body as well as the lower, you can burn up to 800 calories an hour."

Jumping rope can be demanding and frustrating when you are starting out. Many think that it is just too difficult to learn and that a cardiovascular workout will not be attained because they will not be able to keep jumping for 20 minutes. They also think that skipping is simply boring and

Louis Garcia of Los Angeles. World's greatest rope jumper.

few minutes at a time before stopping. Instead of just putting your rope down and stopping when you feel that you just can't continue jumping any longer, put both handles in one hand and continue to execute the jump with the rope turning to the side of the body. At this point you are not jumping inside the rope, but outside of the rope. A two-foot jump or basic jog while continuously turning the rope will keep the heart rate elevated for a length of 20 minutes or more and may reduce the frustration of frequently stopping and starting. Even an accomplished jump roper will use neutral or resting moves to add variety to the cardio-workout and will allow for higher- and lower-intensity training."

The three-step breakdown divides up more complicated moves into manageable moves that can be easily practiced and learned. This systematic training method starts with the footwork being practiced without the rope. In the second step, both handles of the rope are placed into one hand, and the new move is executed while turning the rope at one side, much like the neutral or resting moves. The third step is performing the move inside of the rope. Whenever you have a more challenging foot pattern that you want to perform, the three-step breakdown will help you to succeed.

too repetitive. But there is a lot more to it than just jumping up and down.

FreeStyle roper Louis Garcia believes that jumping rope is something that can be taught to virtually anyone and can be learned within weeks of starting. He has developed a teaching method based on neutral and resting moves and the "three-step breakdown." This teaching method is used successfully in 60- and 30-minute jump rope classes and allows even the novice to feel triumphant.

Garcia explains, "Neutral and resting moves were developed because it is difficult, if not impossible, for beginning jump ropers to continuously jump through (or inside) a rope for more than a

Equipment

A plastic segmented or "beaded" jump rope weighing about a half a pound is the best choice for jumping. It allows the length to be adjusted, customizing it specifically for the height that is required. A rope that is too long or too short will force you to adjust the position of the arms, causing poor execution of movement and jumping technique. And by simply knotting the rope near the handles, you disturb the arc of the rope. A rope that is too light will also not hold a true arc, and it will become more easily tangled and be unable to create a sufficient amount of momentum to produce the desired motion. Conversely, a rope that is too heavy produces slow, cumbersome rotations, increases the risk of injury at the wrists and shoulders, and increases pain on impact when you miss. Look for a rope that has comfortable, durable, and well-constructed handles, perhaps covered in a foam material to help reduce the handle movement in your hands.

Form and Technique: How to Jump

Start with proper form and good technique. Whether you are just starting to jump or you are performing an array of masterful foot and arm movements, there are a few dos and don'ts to remember.

- Jump only an inch or two off the ground.

- Keep the knees slightly bent.

- Land softly on the ground, rolling through the full feet so the legs will absorb the impact.

- Keep the jumps in control with the torso basically straight. Do not allow the body to lean forward or backward.

- Initiate the action of the turning of the rope at the wrist, with little movement at the shoulders or with the arms. A proper weight of rope will assist in reducing shoulder and arm movement.

- Try to keep the shoulders down and relaxed.

- Keep the arms at one level, usually with the upper part of the arms close to the sides of the body. Be careful not to allow the arms to drift away from the body, as this will raise the rope farther from the floor and closer to the jumping feet, resulting in the rope becoming entangled in the feet.

- Keep the head in a neutral position and the neck relaxed.

It does take practice and practice pays off. Within a few weeks you will be putting together foot and arm combinations that will improve your agility, balance and cardiovascular fitness.

Executing a Neutral Move

One of the more difficult challenges in rope jumping is to keep going, and as previously mentioned the neutral move helps you through wanting to just throw the rope down. Keep the feet moving, jump up and down, and place both handles in one hand. The body, shoulders, arms, and wrists should be in proper position (as described in the previous list) as the rope turns at the side of the body. Try not to let the rope wander in front of the body. The purpose is to learn the feel of the rotation and movement of the rope, to keep the feet moving, and to not worry about the rope getting caught in the feet. Change the rope to the other hand once in a while to add variety, as well as to get comfortable with different arm positions. When you start executing arm crossovers while jumping, the positions of the arms will move away from the body, and the movement of the rope will alter. So this is a great place to start feeling the movement.

Jumps and Combinations

The Basic Two-Foot Jump (Difficulty Level 1)

Stand on the floor with the rope behind the feet and both feet side by side. Relax the head and shoulders and face the head straight forward. Keep the arms by the side of the body, hands holding onto the rope comfortably. Push off the floor with the feet, jumping into the air while rotating the

Basic two-foot jump

Boxer's skip

Ski jump right

rope upward behind the back, over the head, in front of the body, and under the feet. Remember to keep the arms by the side of the body and rotate the rope with the wrists. The handles of the rope should always stay the same distance away from the floor. Feet should come only an inch to a half an inch off the floor. (Avoid jumping too high or kicking the feet back.) Land on the balls of the feet and roll through the feet until the full feet are on the floor. Keep the knees slightly bent when landing in order to absorb part of the impact. Repeat, varying the speed to change intensity levels. To start, try to jump between 100 and 140 jumps per minute. The speed of the rope rotations and your height will influence the number of skips per minute performed. A shorter person will most likely be able to perform a greater number of jumps per minute due to the smaller rotation that the rope must travel.

Boxer's Skip (Difficulty Level 1)

Start with the basic two-foot jump and shift your weight from one foot to the other. Keep the knees slightly bent, and push off from one foot at a time. Keep the feet close to the floor, as in the basic two-foot jump. Relax the shoulder and neck. Try to obtain a rhythm from side to side, and vary the footwork slightly: right foot, left foot, two rights; then left foot, right foot, two lefts. Repeat and add in the basic two-foot jump.

Ski Jump (Difficulty Level 2)

Perform the basic two-foot jump while landing to the right side of your starting point and then the left side. When learning this jump it sometimes helps to jump to one side, jump back to the center, then jump to the other side, then back to the center. Repeat until you feel comfortable, then take out the center jump. Remember to keep the arms by the side of the body and rotate the rope at the wrists. With the addition of side-to-side or front-to-back movement, the arms have a tendency to travel outward, which will result in the rope becoming entangled in the feet. Stay cool and relaxed through the shoulder and neck areas and find your rhythm.

Ski jump center

Ski jump left

One-foot kick

One-Foot Kicks (Difficulty Level 2)

Start with the basic two-foot jump. Raise the right foot about six inches off the floor, then perform a basic two-foot jump, then lift the left foot off the floor, then a basic two-foot jump. Try to increase difficulty by traveling forward and backward and lifting the kicking leg higher.

High Knees (Difficulty Level 3)

Start with the boxer's skip and lift the knees higher in front. Ensure that you land softly, rolling through the ball of the foot back to the heel and keeping a slight bend at the knee. Keep the body upright, arms and hands in the proper position. Focus on the push-off phase of one foot, then the other, lifting the knees very high. By practicing this jump, you will help improve not only your cardio-vascular fitness but also the muscle power in each ankle and leg. Try performing 10 to 20 high knees, then perform either a neutral move or boxer's skip to recover your breathing. You may also want to

High knees

add direction into this jump, by traveling forward for 8 jumps and backward for 8 jumps. Ensure that the rope does not stray from the body by keeping the arms close to the side of the body and having proper posture.

forming this jump while rotating the rope, be careful not to make the foot separation too wide, as the rope will most likely get tangled with your feet. The longer the rope, the farther the feet can be separated; the shorter the rope, the tighter the jump.

Jumping Jacks/Stride Jumps (Difficulty Level 3)

Start with a basic two-foot jump, and when in the air separate the feet about shoulder-width. Land with the feet in this position, push off again, and bring the feet back together in the air before landing on the floor with the feet together. When per-

Double Jumps (Difficulty Level 5)

This jump will deposit you right into anaerobic land—two rotations of the rope, one magnified jump! To perform this jump, the rope speed must be faster and the jump in the air must be substantially higher than the basic jump. This is one jump

Jumping jack

Double jump

that will demand both muscular strength and cardiovascular fitness. To start, perform one double jump and five or six basic two-foot jumps. Repeat, trying to reduce the number of basic jumps performed between the double jumps. For a real blast, work up to three sets of twenty double jumps with a neutral move in between the sets.

Crossovers (Difficulty Level 5)

Start with the basic two-foot jump, and when the rope is overhead and coming forward, cross the arms at waist level. The left hand will be at the right hip and the right hand will be at the left hip.

Keep the wrists straight and the rope handles pointing out to the sides, not downward. As the rope comes down toward the toes, jump over it, and as it comes overhead again, uncross the arms. The hands will be at the starting position now. Perform a few basic jumps and repeat the crossover. With just a little practice, crossover jumps can be repeated many times in a row, traveling forward, backward, and in a circle.

Ali Shuffle (Difficulty Level 3)

This is the boxer's jump, with the addition of moving the feet front and back. As you jump in the air,

Crossover jump—start

Crossover jump—finish

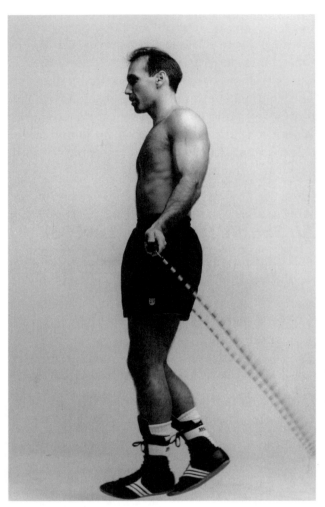

Ali shuffle—start

Ali shuffle—finish

move one foot forward slightly and one foot backward slightly, and then have both land on the floor. Push off the floor again, taking the front foot toward the back and the back foot toward the front, landing with both feet on the floor. Repeat, landing softly and moving quickly. The center of gravity changes slightly as one foot is in front and the other foot is in back, challenging your agility and response time. Muhammad Ali was known for his quick foot movements, shuffling across the canvas from side to side and tiring his opponents. Practicing this jump will teach you to be on your toes,

moving and changing your foot positioning and maintaining a center posture, ready for any directional change.

Ali Shuffle and Jumping Jacks (Difficulty Level 4)

To start working on agility, timing, and balance, combine the Ali shuffle with jumping jacks. Start with eight shuffles, then eight jacks. Reduce down to a single shuffle and a single jack.

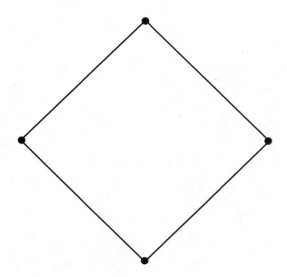

Diamond jump

Diamond Jump (Difficulty Level 4)

Taking the basic two-foot jump, push off both feet, moving six to eight inches to a point on the diamond. Since a single jump is performed at each point of the diamond, this is a great test for agility and leg power. Then change direction and repeat the jumps.

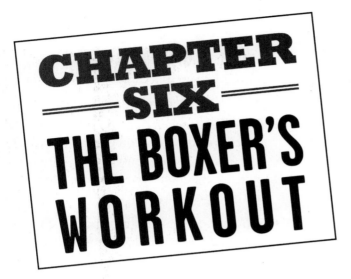

The Program

The boxer's workout pulls everything together. The weight training and cardio-conditioning will assist you during these training days. The power behind your punches on the heavy bag, the slipping and movement around the double-end bag, the muscle endurance needed for the speed bag, and the cardio-conditioning required to last the three-minute rounds are worked on during this training session.

The Warm-Up

To get ready for the boxer's workout, become both mentally and physically prepared. As discussed in Chapter 3, shadow boxing is a great way to warm up the muscles, review the execution of the punches, and prepare yourself mentally to hit the different boxing bags. If a mirror is available, check out your stance, making sure the fists are held near the chin, the elbows are in to protect the body, and the feet and body are in a strong stance. Keep the hands up and move around the floor, side to side, front and back. Add some body movement and head movement. Now add some jabs and straight punches. Move around like you are on the canvas, not only throwing punches, but also getting out of the way of punches that could be thrown at you. Stay loose but in control, and punch with light intent, not thinking about speed or power. Continue for about two minutes, then slowly pick up the tempo, adding a little more bounce in your foot movement, feinting front and back. If you feel tight in any of your muscles, this is a great time to slowly take the limbs through a greater range of motion and lengthen the muscles. The major areas of concern should be the shoulder area, hip flexor, and legs. (Refer to Chapter 7.) Continue the shadow boxing warm-up for about five minutes.

Jump Rope

Start jumping rope at an easy pace. Your body is still going through a warm-up. The footwork should be kept basic and the intensity low for about two minutes. Increase the intensity slightly by either performing more intricate footwork or by increasing the speed at which you are jumping. If you are a seasoned jumper, you may want to try some sprints (around the six-minute mark), performing high knee jogging for 20 to 25 seconds and then bringing the intensity back down for 60 to 90 seconds. Repeat four to six times. Attempt to jump for a total of 12 minutes. This can be accomplished by working up to this time frame, taking a break when needed, or by reducing the intensity until you have built up your stamina. Remember when trying new moves to use the three-step breakdown (see Chapter 5).

Shadow Boxing

Now it's time to get more serious and execute the punches with a little more intent. As with the warm-up, move around, mix up the punches, and keep the heart rate elevated. Working in three-minute rounds, with one minute of rest in between, have a game plan of what punches and punch combinations you want to tackle. Develop both offensive moves and defensive moves. This is when you want to be creative and also work on transitions that do not feel comfortable and smooth. During shadow boxing, the punching technique, balance, weight transfers from foot to foot, and combinations can be developed and corrected. Get a feel for the three-minute time limit, and pace yourself so that you are working at about 60 to 70 percent of your maximum effort. During the one-minute rest, take time to prepare for the next three-minute round. Ask yourself what punches felt smooth and under control and what movements did and did not flow well, and develop a game plan.

Follow these guidelines to match your shadow rounds with your skill level:

- *Beginner*: Perform the straight punches: the jab and the straight right power punch. Concentrate on the punch execution and placement of the arms, the wrists, and the body. Add some footwork and punch

combinations, and focus mainly on the technique of the punches until they become second nature.

- *Intermediate*: Perform a greater variety of punches and punch combinations, adding footwork and body movement. Also increase the intensity by adding a bounce to the movement.

- *Advanced*: Perform the same movement as intermediate, but hold onto small weights (one-half to two pounds). Work at 70 percent intensity, promoting the development of muscular and punching endurance. Use your imagination, and work on both attacking and retreating moves.

NOTE: For a balanced fitness workout, practice the punches on both the right side and the left (orthodox and southpaw stance).

Hitting the Heavy Bag

Three different intensity levels are described from beginner to more advanced. Choose the one that is best suited to your fitness level and experience.

Level One

This is a great place to start to learn the feeling and the technique behind hitting a heavy bag. By performing repetition after repetition of a single punch, the movement and execution will become second nature. This will set you up for adding movement and combinations so they flow easily. Start punching for a total of one and a half minutes, working up to three minutes for all three rounds. Rest between each round, 45 seconds for one-and-a-half-minute rounds and one minute for three-minute rounds.

Follow these guidelines for the three-round session:

- *Round One*—This round is a "range finder" and allows you to get the feel of hitting the bag and the power behind the punches. Standing in the classic boxing stance, practice your left jab for half of the round time. Switch your stance and repeat your right jab for the same amount of time.

- *Round Two*—Standing in the classic boxing stance, practice your right power punch for half of the round time. Switch your stance and repeat your left power punch for the same amount of time.

- *Round Three*—Standing in the orthodox boxing stance, practice the one-two punch (jab, power punch) for half the round. Switch your stance and repeat in the southpaw stance for the same amount of time. For example: the one-two punch combination—a left jab followed by a straight right in rapid succession. Slip and move and repeat. The majority of punch combinations should start with the jab.

NOTE: If the arms fatigue quickly, do not risk injury at the joint areas (shoulders, elbows, and wrists). Switch your stance from side to side. As you build muscle strength and endurance, you will increase the length of punching time.

Level Two

In this level you should feel comfortable working on the bag performing the basic punches. Put together combinations, adding body movement and footwork. This will increase the intensity of the workout. Start with two-minute rounds, increasing to three-minute rounds. For a two-minute round, rest 45 seconds, and for a three-minute round, rest one minute. Keep moving and walk around during the rest period. Focus on the next round.

These guidelines match the skill level with the typical three-round session:

- *Round One*—Punch the bag with straight punches, jabs, and power-punch combinations. Move around, work on balance, and incorporate footwork.

- *Round Two*—Repeat round one, but punch with more intent. Add slips, feint right and left, and stay on the toes. For example: jab, power punch, slip, jab, power punch. Double jab, move away from the bag, move toward the bag, and finish with a one-two punch.

- *Round Three*—Add some hooks to the combinations. For example: one-two hook combination—step into the bag as you launch your left jab followed by a straight right. You should now be in position to throw a short left hook to finish the combination. Step away and circle the bag as you plan your next sequence of punches.

NOTE: Become aware of your timing and find your own rhythm. Maintain a center of balance when you make contact with the bag with a maximum hit.

Level Three

Once you have the punches down, work on the bag like you are in the ring. Add more movement, have a strategy (game plan), and work in hooks, uppercuts with jabs, and power punches. Mix it all up. Hit the bag for three-minute rounds and rest for one minute.

For the most intense three-round session, follow these guidelines:

- *Round One*—This warm-up round. Throw a lot of straight punches and move around. Work on a single technique to perfect punching power or a combination to develop smooth transitions from one punch to the next. Work at 60 to 70 percent of full intensity.

- *Round Two*—Add more power and intent to the punches. Snap your punches.

- *Round Three*—Remember, nothing stays still in the boxing ring, so keep moving, change direction, and use the heavy bag to your advantage. Work your punches in bunches.

Heavy-Bag Speed Sprints

An advanced punching workout on the heavy bag, sprints are a succession of fast punches over spec-ified periods of time. The purpose is to increase punch speed, work the arm and back muscles for power and endurance, and challenge the cardiorespiratory system. This workout imitates the demands placed on the body in a fight situation, when nearing the end of a round you feel too tired to lift your arms.

Address the bag straight on, not in a boxing stance, so the arms have equal reach and contact on the bag. Maintain this reach distance. Keep the feet stationary, and hold the body core tight. Shift the body weight slightly forward, standing on the balls

Address the bag square.

Deliver straight punches, no hooks.

of the feet, and relax the knees. This will give you power and help you focus on throwing the punches with speed. Throw straight punches, not hooks, in a one-two rhythm. The sprint times are short, so put a lot of effort into your punches. Keep breathing throughout the sprints, and punch as fast as you can.

Start with 15-second sprints, working up to 25-second sprints. It is best to have a timer. Always rest the same amount of time as you work. Walk around and think about your next sprint. Repeat three to four more times.

Throw punches as quickly as possible.

Target Mitts (Optional)

If you have a partner, train with the target mitts. Concentrate on the execution of the punches, work for three three-minute rounds. Keep the more intense power punches for the heavy bag. (Refer to Chapter 3 for sample punch combinations.)

Cool-Down Round

The purpose of the cool-down is to decrease the heart rate, to take the muscle and joint areas through a full range of motion, and to review the punches. If you have a speed bag and double-end bag available, this is a great time to work out on them. Refer to Chapter 4 for information on speed-bag and double-end-bag training. End with shadow boxing for three to six minutes, punching with light intent rather than focusing on power. Stay light on your feet, shrugging and rotating the shoulders. Let the muscles relax.

Abdominal Workout

Now that the heart rate has decreased, lie on the floor and perform the abdominal exercises as described in Chapter 8. Concentrate on the contraction of the abdominal muscles, lifting the body and then lowering the body back to the floor with control.

Cool-Down/Stretches

The stretches are described in Chapter 7. After every workout, perform stretching and relaxation exercises. This will help lengthen the muscle tissue and reduce soreness the next day.

NOTE: If you are traveling and do not have access to any equipment, try "The One-Two Punch" fitness video available at www.theonetwo punch.com.

THE BOXER'S WORKOUT

WARM-UP ROUND
Shadow box and perform light stretching for five minutes.

JUMP ROPE
Warm-up: Jump easily for two to three minutes.
Jump: Keep jumping, performing different moves for ten to twelve minutes.
(Refer to Chapter 5.)

SHADOW BOXING
Choose the beginner, intermediate, or advanced level and work up to three three-minute rounds.
Round One: Practice the basic punches focusing on technique and execution.
Round Two: Move around more while practicing the punches and combinations.
Round Three: Add more intent to the punches, and work on combinations.

HEAVY BAG
Choose the appropriate level to work at according to your fitness level and experience.
Work the punches on the heavy bag for three minutes and rest for one minute in between. Perform three rounds.

HEAVY-BAG SPEED SPRINTS
Face the heavy bag straight on, check your arm reach, relax the legs, keep the body core tight, and start punching. Remember to rest the same length of time as the sprint.

Sprint 1: 15 to 20 seconds	Rest: 15 to 20 seconds
Sprint 2: 15 to 20 seconds	Rest: 15 to 20 seconds
Sprint 3: 15 to 20 seconds	Rest: 15 to 20 seconds
Sprint 4: 15 to 20 seconds (optional)	

TARGET MITTS (OPTIONAL)
If you have a partner, train with the target mitts. Concentrate on the punches, working for three three-minute rounds.

COOL-DOWN ROUND
Shadow box lightly, move around, and review the punches. Practice on the double-end bag and speed bag if available. Cool down for three to six minutes.

ABDOMINAL WORKOUT
Refer to Chapter 8, "Muscle Conditioning."

COOL-DOWN/STRETCHES
Refer to Chapter 7, "Cardio-Conditioning." Spend five to ten minutes performing these exercises.

"BOXING SHORTS"
A 30-MINUTE MAINTENANCE WORKOUT

There are times when you may not have the time for a full workout, or after completing the 12-week program you may feel like a change. Try the 30-minute maintenance workout, "Boxing Shorts." It allows you to maintain your existing fitness level in a shorter workout, but still allows you to throw plenty of punches. The Boxing Shorts workout should not replace the boxer's workout on a continual basis, but it is great for a change. It is rigorous and invigorating, and it challenges the cardiovascular and muscular systems.

Keep moving from exercise to exercise, staying focused and not taking any breaks. The program design is short enough for anyone with a busy schedule.

WARM-UP (THREE MINUTES)
Start with easy warm-up shadow boxing with light hand weights, not any greater than two pounds. If you have a speed bag, work for two to three minutes on it. Take the muscles and joints of the arms and legs through an optimal range of motion. Wrap your hands.

JUMP ROPE (THREE MINUTES)
Jump rope, keeping a good jumping rate and lifting the knees high. Try some varied footwork.

HEAVY BAG (FIVE MINUTES)
The body has most likely adapted to the three-minute rounds. By increasing the length of time boxing, you place an overload on the muscles and energy sources. To really increase the workout, try to hit the bag at a three-minute pace for five minutes.

JUMP ROPE (FIVE MINUTES)
Keep the pace of jumping fairly fast. Perform some sprints and double jumps to elevate the heart rate.

HEAVY BAG (FIVE MINUTES)
Punch with intent, work the bag, and move around.

SHADOW BOX (THREE MINUTES)
Keep moving for the first minute, then slow down, letting the heart rate lower and the breathing rate return to normal.

ABDOMINAL WORKOUT (FOUR MINUTES)
Perform abdominal exercises with the medicine ball. Refer to Chapter 8, "Muscle Conditioning."

COOL-DOWN/STRETCHES (TWO MINUTES)
Perform stretches and flexibility exercises, as described in Chapter 7.

THE CHAMP'S WORKOUT

If you have successfully been training in the boxer's workout, Level Three, then give the Champ's Workout a try!

WARM-UP ROUND

Perform light shadow boxing with zero intent for three minutes. Move the limbs through a range of motion, warming up the muscles.

JUMP ROPE

Jump rope for twelve to twenty minutes.
Warm-up: easy jumping for two minutes
Jump: normal rate for two to four minutes
Sprint: 20 double jumps
Jump: normal rate for two to four minutes
Sprint: 30 double jumps
Jump: normal rate for two to four minutes
Sprint: 40 double jumps
Jump: easy jumping for two to four minutes
NOTE: If you have not mastered double jumps, perform high knees at a faster pace.

SHADOW BOXING

Use hand weights one-half pound to two pounds. Never shadow box with more than two-pound weights. Perform three-minute rounds for four rounds.
Round One: Practice the basic punches focusing on technique and execution.
Round Two: Put combinations together, adding head movement and developing fluidity between the punches and combinations.
Round Three: Work on more combinations with foot and head movement.
Round Four: Do not use weights. Work all the punches together and add a lot of footwork.

HEAVY-BAG SPEED SPRINTS

Face the heavy bag straight on, check the reach of the arms, relax the legs, and get ready to work hard. Remember to rest, walking around the same length of time as the sprint.

Sprint 1: 40 seconds	Rest: 40 seconds
Sprint 2: 40 seconds	Rest: 40 seconds
Sprint 3: 30 seconds	Rest: 30 seconds
Sprint 4: 30 seconds	Rest: 30 seconds
Sprint 5: 20 seconds	Rest: 20 seconds
Sprint 6: 20 seconds	Rest: 20 seconds

HEAVY BAG

Mix up the punches, add footwork, and work on combinations over and over and over again for four rounds. Work for three minutes and rest for one minute.

TARGET MITTS (OPTIONAL)

If you have a partner, train with the target mitts. Concentrate on the punches. Work for three three-minute rounds.

COOL-DOWN ROUND

Train on the speed bag and the double-end bag for three minutes each. Shadow box for three minutes, throwing punches with no intent.

ABDOMINAL WORKOUT

Refer to Chapter 8 for the abdominal exercises. Include some of the medicine ball abdominal exercises.

COOL-DOWN/STRETCHES

Refer to Chapter 7. Always stretch after each workout.

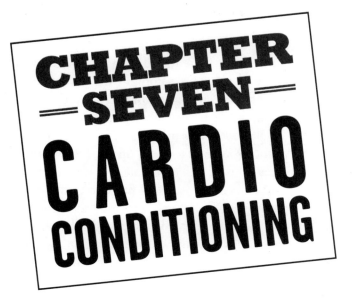

CHAPTER SEVEN
CARDIO CONDITIONING

People were designed to move, to place one foot in front of the other, to develop their muscles and expand their physical and mental capabilities. Running is a great avenue to learn about how you move, to feel the leg and gluteal muscles working, the heart pumping, the breath entering the body, the sweat building on the skin and then dripping to the ground.

Running allows you to get outdoors and become part of this great world. It can be done just about anywhere and with very little equipment or experience. Just a pair of shoes and the desire to move your body from one place to another are all that is needed. Running can be done in a group and can be a very social activity, or it can be performed on an individual basis. The training is specific to each individual, and you will find your preferred routes, time of day, speed, and tempo.

The significance of the cardio-conditioning days in the One-Two Punch Boxing Workout is to improve the ability of the heart and lungs to adapt to the external demands of the body moving faster and harder. If you prefer not to or are unable to run outdoors, then substitute the time on indoor cardio equipment, such as a treadmill, stair-climbing machine, or stationary bike. You could also use your jump rope at a moderate pace. If you

have an injury, replace the cardio-conditioning days with an activity that will increase your heart rate and breathing rate for the recommended length of time, like riding a stationary bike or swimming in a pool.

Why and How a Boxer Does It

Both the cardiorespiratory and vascular systems must be trained in order to "go the distance" in a boxing round. Depending on whether the fight is an amateur or a professional fight, and assuming no one is knocked out in the first few rounds, the boxer has to keep moving from 12 minutes to 40 minutes.

To build the necessary stamina, boxers will usually train their cardio systems by running, jogging, jumping rope, and hitting the bag. The road-work portion of their training involves running or jogging long distances at a relatively moderate pace, usually outdoors. Roadwork training is generally performed three to four times per week, with the intention of building stamina to stay strong through the entire bout.

Start with roadwork (or the equivalent on a bike, treadmill, or stair-climbing machine) to condition the aerobic capacity of your body. As you become more adapted to the distance and pace of the roadwork, the cardiorespiratory and vascular systems will improve. More demands can then be placed on the body during the training in order to develop an even higher level of fitness.

Traditionally, cardio-training for boxers included long runs and also interval training of sparring with a partner in the ring. The long runs trained the cardio-aerobic system, the system that utilizes oxygen as the source of energy to perform the activity and allows an activity to be continued for an extended period of time. Working in the ring and sparring with a partner accomplished the training for the cardio-anaerobic system. The anaerobic system requires glucose, adenosine triphosphate (ATP), and creatine phosphate (CP) as the energy sources to perform the activity and provide quick, strong movements for shorter periods of time. This type of activity can be performed only in short spurts or intervals and is known as interval training.

Long runs, skipping, and sparring with a partner in the ring were the accepted methods to train the cardiorespiratory and vascular systems—that is until recently! Many are now realizing the importance of imitating the demands of the three-minute round by performing running sprints during roadwork and by interval training outside of the ring. Remember, a two- or three-minute round places specific demands on the body, very different from the demands of lasting a bout. And the body has to be trained to respond to the faster and more intense demands of a round, as well as to the extensive demands of an entire bout.

The Program

Part of the cardio-conditioning program will include training for endurance—to go the distance—and the long run will be an essential part of this program. It is important to note that these long runs serve as the foundation for overall conditioning and must be accomplished before moving on to the interval sprint work. During the continuous training, the objective is to sustain an aerobic activity for 20 to 60 minutes. The intensity level you want to work at to build up your endurance should be at a lower and moderate intensity level for safety and comfort reasons. When the body's stamina is improved, fatigue will result less often, and the chance of injury will be reduced. The physical condition of the body will then develop to a base level of fitness that allows greater physical demands to be placed on it.

Once this base level of conditioning is achieved, then interval training can be incorporated into the cardio-conditioning program. Interval training is repeated periods of higher-intensity exercise that last 15 to 30 seconds. By placing these demands on the heart and the musculature, the body is being trained to withstand a three-minute round in the ring. Interval training is a great way to improve the anaerobic power and speed of the conditioned athlete, but because of the faster movements and high contractile force of the muscle fibers, there is a greater probability of musculoskeletal injury. Also, the body will produce more lactic acid as a by-product of the higher-intensity movement, and this may cause discomfort in the muscles, making you want to quit the activity. Keep your interval training workouts short to start, and become familiar with how it feels to work at the higher intensity.

The cardio-conditioning days are Day 2 and Day 4, and the workout session should last for 30 minutes to one hour. Depending on your base fitness level, the program may be started with a walk/jog program, increasing up to a full jog, run, and sprint program.

Equipment
Footwear

The most important purchase that you will make is a functional and comfortable pair of running shoes. The shoe protects and supports the foot and improves traction when running. There are a variety of styles and brand names to choose from today, and you're sure to find a fit that is specific to your lifestyle and running style. The shoe should have sufficient support for your weight and adequate sole cushioning. Good heel support and midsole flexibility are two important factors to look for in a running shoe. Visit a store that has a knowledgeable and trained staff, try on different styles, and make an educated purchase.

Clothing

As a rule of thumb, in hot weather wear light-colored cotton or breathable fabrics that are loose fitting. In cold weather, try to dress in layers and cover the head, face, and hands. A great investment to make is in clothing that has moisture-transport capabilities. The high-tech fibers in the clothes allow perspiration (water vapor) to evaporate away from the skin and out through the material but do not allow rain droplets to soak into the material. Some of the fabrics combine water repellency, windproofing, and warming properties for colder outside training.

Measuring Training Intensities

To start a running program it is necessary to learn how to measure the level at which you are working. There are a few methods that are standard to the fitness industry and easily applied to cardio-conditioning. The heart rate and talk test are two ways to measure how hard you are working.

The Heart Rate

The heart beats a specific number of times per minute, and this number is unique to each individual. When the body starts to move during activity, the heart muscle must pump more blood more often to provide sufficient quantities of oxygen to the muscle tissue. A trained heart pumps out a greater volume of blood and does not need to beat as often to provide the necessary oxygen to the body, whether at rest or while exercising. Many factors such as age, heredity, and sex cannot be altered, but your fitness level can. As your cardio-conditioning improves, your heart rate will decrease so there are a fewer number of beats per minute.

How to Take Your Pulse

To take your resting heart rate without equipment, sit in a comfortable position and find either your carotid artery (in the neck region) or your radial artery (on the inside of the wrist). The pulse in the neck area is found by gently placing the index finger or the middle finger over the lower neck, just above the collarbone. It is important to not press too hard, as arteries are pressure sensitive and the heart rate may actually drop. The radial pulse in the wrist can be found by placing the index and middle fingers on the underside of the wrist and the thumb on the top of the wrist. Once again, press lightly.

To measure your heart rate when exercising, reduce your intensity and find your pulse. Press lightly and count for a specific length of time, somewhere between 10 and 60 seconds. The longer you take the read, the more accurate is the heart rate count. You will want to calculate the number of beats per minute. If you count for 10 seconds, then multiply the number by six; if you take a 30-second count, then multiply by two. The longer 60-second count is the most precise; however, to count for 60 seconds means that you will have to reduce your activity during the time, interfering with your workout.

Heart Rate Monitors

Today digital heart rate monitors, usually incorporated into a training watch or stopwatch, are available at most sporting-goods stores. A special electrode sensor is placed on the arm or the chest and picks up the signal of the heart beating. These are great devices because you do not have to stop exercising to take a pulse, and readings are generally accurate. Excessive motion of where the electrode is making contact, though, may produce inaccurate readings. Also, other electromagnetic systems may interfere with the heart signal.

The Resting Heart Rate

The resting heart rate is a good indicator of your basic fitness level and is a great starting place to learn about your fitness level. Just before you get up out of bed in the morning, count the number of times that your heart beats in one minute. This number is known as your resting heart rate and is the base measurement indicator to determine improvements in your fitness level. As your fitness level improves, the resting heart rate will decrease, and this means that the heart does not have to pump as many times per minute to provide the body with oxygen-rich blood.

The Training Heart Rate

The training heart rate is a number range in which the heart should be beating in order to produce a conditioning effect. To obtain a training effect on the heart muscle, a general rule of thumb is to maintain a heart rate that is between 60 and 75 percent of your maximum heart rate. One method of calculating the maximum heart rate is by subtracting your age from 220. Therefore, if you are 30 years old, your maximum heart rate will be 220 minus 30, or 190 beats in 60 seconds. Sixty percent of the maximum heart rate will give the lower heart rate number for the training heart rate. In our example, 60 percent of 190 beats equals 114 beats per minute. Seventy-five percent of the maximum heart rate will give you the higher end of the training heart rate, or 75 percent of 190 beats equals 142 beats in a minute. The training heart rate would therefore be 114 beats to 142 beats per minute (a 19- to 24-beat count in 10 seconds.)

The intensity level at which you train should be specific to you individually and is dependent on both your own capabilities and the type of exercise that is being performed. Ensure that the level you work at exceeds mild physical demand but does not produce extreme breathlessness, fatigue, or confusion.

During cardio-conditioning, as the heart is trained, the heart rate readings over a period of training weeks should decrease. Let's say that during week one, after 20 minutes of roadwork, the heart rate count for 60 seconds was 140 beats per minute. In week four, performing exactly the same route and time duration, the heart rate may be reduced to 138 to 135 beats per minute. Generally, a decrease of 4 to 10 beats per minute can be expected after a six- to eight-week training period. A less fit individual will see a greater difference, whereas a well-conditioned athlete will see less of a difference. Some variables such as age, initial fitness level, length of training program, and program intensity will influence the training results.

The method you select to determine your heart rate should be consistent from workout to workout so that comparisons are valid. Many factors may influence your heart rate from day to day such as stress level, digestion, biological rhythms, temperature, and your health status. The heart rate measure should be only a guide when assessing the differences in your cardio-fitness level over a period of time.

The "Talk Test" Measure of Exercising Intensity

An easy way to measure how hard you are working is to use the "talk test." This is a very subjective measure of the workout intensity and can be very useful in determining the comfort zone of aerobic intensity. To determine your talking threshold, increase your activity until it is difficult to talk and breathe comfortably. This is the talking threshold. You want to be just below this level. The aim is to breathe rhythmically and comfortably throughout all phases of the workout. As you progress to higher functional capacities and higher workout levels, the talk test is a conservative measure, especially at more than 80 percent of the functional capacity. It is more accurate to use the heart rate monitor.

Cardio-Conditioning Workout
The Warm-Up

It is important to warm up before starting any running program. A great way to increase the blood flow in the body is to warm up by shadow boxing—moving side to side and forward and backward and throwing punches. You can also warm up by walking for five minutes at a fairly good pace, swinging the arms and stretching out the muscles if they feel tight. Do not do full flexibility stretches until you are completely warmed up, preferably after the run.

Initial Conditioning Level—Just Starting Out

Begin by walking (two to five minutes) and jogging (two to five minutes), intermittently for a total of 12 to 15 minutes. Try to work at 60 to 75 percent of your maximum heart rate or use the talk test, remembering that you should be able to talk while still breathing heavily. Your goal is to increase the total length of time of the walk and jog to 30 to 45 minutes. Initially walk and jog in equal intervals and then gradually increase the jogging interval to be longer than the walking interval. This initial conditioning stage may last between four and six weeks, sometimes longer.

Intermediate Conditioning Level—Improvement Stage

If you are currently involved in an exercise program or are comfortable running for 20 minutes continuously, then you are at a level where you will be able to improve your running speed and distance over the next eight to twenty weeks. By gradually increasing the jogging distance and the speed, you are training the heart to be able to handle greater physical stresses. The heart should be working at 60 to 85 percent of the maximum heart rate. The exercise duration or the time that you spend jogging should be increased every two to three weeks. (Gradually increase the jogging distance or energy expenditure to the desired distance or time.) You want to work up to continuous running/jogging for 45 minutes to one hour.

Once you are comfortable with continuous training, then you can add interval training on your cardio-conditioning days. Include a few sprints in the fifth cardio-conditioning workout and every fourth workout after that. Remember, you want to increase the heart rate to about 85 percent to 90 percent of your maximum heart rate or work at a level just above the talk-test threshold. Always start with a 10-minute jog/run, then add a 20- to 30-second sprint. Slow down the pace again to your initial speed for one to three minutes and repeat the cycle of sprinting and jogging for three to five times. Finish off with a slower-paced 5- to 10-minute jog.

Advanced Conditioning Level—Maintenance Stage

This is the stage where you are comfortable working in both continuous and interval training, and it is usually reached after the first six months of working out. As your jogging distance increases and your cardiorespiratory endurance improves, increase your stride frequency or the rate at which you place each foot on the ground. Run faster. Run farther. The workout should last for 30 to 60 minutes, working at a level of 75 to 85 percent of your maximum heart rate.

Flexibility and Stretching

For each joint area, the muscles, tendons, ligaments, and bone-on-bone connections are able to achieve a certain degree of movement. This is known as the range of motion. And for each movement, activity, or sport there is an optimal range of motion required to produce the desired outcome. Activities such as ballet will require a far greater range of motion at the hip joint and through the muscles of the legs, whereas activities such as running or boxing would require less in these areas.

Reduced flexibility of the muscles and at the joints can lead to a number of problems, both during training and during normal daily activity, and can be the cause of injury, pain, and discomfort. Muscular imbalance and a misalignment of the muscle fibers can be created both by sports-specific demands making some muscles too tight and inflexible and by poor postural habits. There must always be a balance in the strength of a muscle and the extensibility of that same muscle. A strong muscle that is pliable and limber withstands stress from activity better than a strong, rigid, inflexible muscle. Poor posture may cause muscles to be tightened and shortened, creating problems in associated joints. For example, a lot of running without stretching afterward may reduce the flexibility at the hip joint, reducing the length of the hip flexor muscles, thereby overpowering a weak lower back. Pain will be felt in the lower back and possibly generating down into the back of the legs. By stretching out the hip flexor area and strengthening the lower back and abdominal area, the pain and mus-

cle imbalance can be corrected. Daily stretching promotes the proper alignment of the muscle tissue, lengthening muscles that are tight, inflexible and overused, whether from training, overuse, or poor postural habits. As the range of motion is increased at the joint area, performance can be optimized and the risk of injury greatly reduced.

The degree of flexibility is specific to each individual. Tendon and ligament length, genetics, the elasticity within the muscle tissue, and lifestyle are all determinants of the degree to which you can stretch. Stretch whenever your muscles feel tight, and take the joint through an optimal range of motion. There are two different types of stretching: a static stretch and a dynamic stretch. When performing a static stretch, you lengthen and hold the muscle for a specified amount of time. It is a very controlled stretch with very little visible movement. A dynamic stretch elongates the muscle to a certain length while moving. This type of stretch is still very controlled, but visible movement does occur while the muscle is being stretched. Of course, there is a higher risk of tearing muscle fibers when performing dynamic stretches, and care must be taken to be in control and not bounce or jar into a position (a ballistic stretch).

A preactivity stretch or warm-up stretch is an easy stretch that is aimed at taking the muscle and joints through a full range of motion imitating the movements of the activity to follow. Often it is a dynamic stretch that increases the blood flow to the working muscles, preparing the muscles for activity and initiating neuromuscular coordination. This stretch can be held for 10 to 15 seconds, reducing muscle tightness and warming up the muscle tissue for activity. The purpose is not to increase the muscle in total length.

The postactivity stretch or the developmental lengthening stretch is aimed at relaxing the muscle and lengthening the working muscles to normal length after the repetitive contractions of the muscles during the activity. This is also the time that muscles can be lengthened beyond what is normal for the individual to improve flexibility. Stretching will also promote the removal of workout waste by-products (like lactic acid) in the blood and muscle mass and provide new nutrients to rebuild the muscle tissue. Slow, static stretching is effective in reducing the localized muscle soreness after exercising and will assist in increasing the amount and the quality of synovial fluid that is available at the joint areas, making movement freer and easier at the bone-on-bone connection. Postexercise stretching is also a great time to make improvements in your muscle extensibility and length. After the workout, the body and muscle temperature is elevated and the risk of tearing a muscle fiber or the connective tissue is reduced. By stretching on a regular basis, improvements in muscle length are very noticeable and beneficial to performance. A postactivity stretch is held for 10 to 30 seconds,

holding the stretch at a point where tension is felt, relaxing, and then moving a fraction further into the stretch.

Remember that stretching is noncompetitive and should be performed in a relaxed environment. It has a way of promoting a sense of well-being and will increase your awareness of your body and musculature.

Do not bounce into a stretch. Using force will not increase the flexibility; it only causes the stretch reflex impulse to contract the muscle fibers, resulting in microscopic tearing of the muscle fibers. This in turn reduces the elasticity of the muscle, and soreness and tightness will result. Also, do not overstretch. It is far better to understretch than overstretch a muscle. Try to find the point where you feel the stretch and are able to relax at the same time. Relaxing the muscle tissue and performing the stretches on a regular basis are the two most important factors in improving your flexibility.

It is important to maintain good flexibility throughout your life. Flexibility decreases with the aging process, and joint stiffness, muscle tightening, decreased range of motion, and poor posture result. Stretching helps to keep the body limber, making activity and movement easier.

Stretching Exercises
Standing Quadriceps/ Hip Flexor Stretch

Stand on one leg, knees together. Lift one leg back, keeping the knees together, and hold onto the ankle or lower leg with the arm on the same side. Stand tall, with the torso held tight, and pull the heel up toward the seat. You should feel a slight stretch in the front leg or quadriceps muscle. To stretch the hip flexor, press the hips forward slightly while keeping the knees together and bending the supporting leg slightly. Hold for 10 to 30

Standing quadricep/hip flexor stretch

Standing calf/achilles stretch

seconds and repeat. Perform five to seven times on each side.

Standing Calf/Achilles Stretch

Stand with one leg forward, one leg back. With both feet facing straight forward, bend the front leg and shift the body toward the front foot. Keep the back heel on the floor. You will feel a stretch in the center of the calf muscle. To stretch the Achilles tendon and the lower part of the calf, bend the back knee slightly, shift the body weight backward just a bit, and keep the back heel on the floor. Hold for 10 to 30 seconds and repeat. Perform five to seven times on each side.

Hamstring Stretch

Sit on the floor comfortably with one leg extended and one leg bent in toward the body. Flex the foot of the extended leg upright and bend forward from the hips, keeping the back as flat as possible. Reach forward only to the point where you are still able to feel relaxed and feel a stretch at the back of the extended leg. Hold for ten to thirty seconds and repeat. Stretch five to seven times on each side.

Upper-Back Stretch

Sit or stand with the arms extended in front of the body. Hold the hands together with the fingers

Hamstring stretch

interlaced and the palms facing away from the body. Then press the hands and arms forward from the shoulder region and allow the back to round. You should feel this stretch is throughout the upper back. Hold for 10 to 30 seconds and repeat three to five times.

Chest and Shoulder Stretch (Pectoral)

Stand tall with the knees relaxed, abdominal muscles tight, arms extended behind the back, and the fingers interlaced. Straighten the arms by rotating the elbows inward, then lift the arms up behind you slightly, stretching through the shoulders, chest, and arms. Hold the stretch for 5 to 15 seconds and repeat three to five times.

Shoulder and Middle of Upper Back (Rhomboideus) Stretch

Stand or sit with one arm crossed in front of the body. Hold onto this arm, and gently press the elbow across the chest to the opposite shoulder, stretching the middle of the upper back. To stretch more of the shoulder area, extend and lower the arm across the body. Hold each stretch for 5 to 15 seconds and repeat three to five times on each side.

Triceps and Shoulder Stretch

Stand or sit tall with the head facing straight forward and both arms held overhead. Hold onto one elbow with the opposite hand and gently press the other hand down the center of the back. Hold for

Upper back stretch

Chest and shoulder stretch

10 to 15 seconds and repeat three to five times on each side.

Some Standard Precautions

Meals

Try not to train the cardio system for at least 90 minutes after a full meal. A large meal will require the heart to pump blood and oxygen to the stomach and the intestines to assist in the digestion of the food. When you start to exercise, the heart then must pump blood to the working muscles, leaving less oxygen available for the brain and the digestion of the food. The result can be nausea, gastric discomfort, increased stress on the heart muscle, and an ineffective workout. The length of time between a meal and a cardio workout is specific to the amount of food eaten and the intensity of the workout. The larger the meal, the longer you should wait before you run.

Environmental Stress

Hot Weather

Reduce your exercise intensity if you are training in very hot or humid weather conditions or at altitudes above 5,000 feet sea level. Wear comfortable, loose-fitting clothing and the appropriate sunscreen. Avoid training during the hottest part of the day, and stay out of direct sunlight if possible.

Shoulder and middle of upper back stretch

Triceps and shoulder stretch

Drink water before, during, and after exercising, four to six ounces in 20-minute intervals. Remember to maintain the training heart rate as your working heart rate will increase faster because of the heat. Reduce your exercising intensity. You may not be running as far or as fast as usual, but you are working just as hard.

Cold Weather

During the cold weather of winter, wear the appropriate thermal clothing and layer it. Keep the hands, fingers, and head covered. Wear sunscreen and sunglasses to protect the face and the eyes from the glare of the snow-covered ground. Avoid training outside on windy and icy days or in temperatures below minus 10 degrees Celsius or 15 degrees Fahrenheit.

Pollution

Be aware of the pollution index and consider training indoors when it is too high, especially if you have any upper respiratory weaknesses.

Illness

Strenuous cardio-exercising should be avoided with flu or upper respiratory tract infections. If you are on prescription medications or over-the-counter medicine, consult with your doctor as to whether there are any contraindications of the medicine when combined with moderate or intense physical activity.

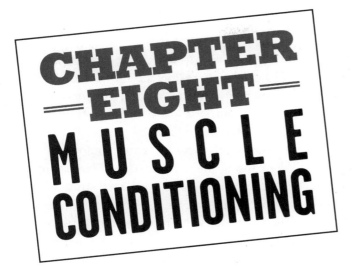

CHAPTER EIGHT
MUSCLE CONDITIONING

At one time, weight training was not included in the boxer's workout regimen. It was felt that weight training would produce a muscle-bound, slower-moving boxer in the ring and that bag work, roadwork, and sparring were sufficient training to increase speed and punching power. But as some of the more recent boxers have discovered, weight training better prepares you for the battle in the ring. It puts power into the punches and stability into the stance, and it reduces the occurrences of joint and muscle injuries. Weight training increases overall stamina, punching and leg speed, and lean body mass and develops the torso to be able to absorb body punches. Professional boxers of the modern era, like Oscar De La Hoya, Evander Holyfield, and Fernando Vargas, believe that strength training is essential to the whole training package, contributing to the overall outcome.

The muscles give the body form. They produce movement by receiving and responding to orders from the brain and central nervous system. Each one of us is in control of sending information to the muscle fibers so that the muscles may produce movement. With specific training, the muscles learn how to respond faster and more efficiently and effectively to specific demands. With continual repetition of a movement, the muscle fiber instinc-

tively performs the movement requested. When we perform and demand the very best and the very extreme from each movement, the muscle fiber increases in strength and circumference with an improved outcome—a greater muscle mass.

The Program

The most efficient and positive method to improve strength and develop muscle tissue is to weight train. Weight training has to be recognized as an important facet of total fitness and is incorporated in the One-Two Punch Boxing Workout twice a week. On Day 3 and Day 6 of the program, 45 minutes to 60 minutes are spent on training a variety of the muscles that are specific to improving boxing movements.

You may wonder why this program suggests training with weights only twice a week, when traditionally bodybuilders train six days a week. Bodybuilders train specific muscle groups twice a week and will have three different workouts, giving six workout days. A lot of time is spent training very specific muscle groups in each session, and the different muscle groups are worked only twice a week. In the workout, all the muscle groups are worked in the one session, two times per week. The emphasis is on using weight training to supplement the overall workout program, promoting improved capabilities for the boxing workout. The program encourages muscular strength and endurance, which in turn provide the basis for stronger and more powerful punches. Improvements in speed, technique, agility, and response time will result from lifting weights.

The purpose of the muscle-conditioning workout will be to develop muscular strength and endurance of the upper and lower body to complement the boxing training. Traditionally, when training with weights, 8 to 12 repetitions of an exercise are performed, and this is repeated three times.

Our goal is to provide a program that will give you strength gains in the least amount of time. The method of weight training used here will be based on lifting a specified weight a maximum of 10 times in the second set of the exercise routine, while the 11th lift cannot be completed. This "max 10 rep" is the basis for setting the weight used in the first set and the third set.

In the first set, the goal is to lift the weight more than 10 repetitions (around 12 repetitions). This is usually around 80 percent of the weight used for the max 10 rep. In the second set, the weight is increased so that the muscle will fatigue at 10 repetitions. In the third set, the weight is reduced to the same weight as used in the first set, and the weight is lifted as many times as possible until total muscle failure results.

If you have trained with weights previously, it should be easy to determine your max 10 rep. If you are new to weight training, start with a lighter weight, perhaps lifting the weight 12 to 14 repetitions. If you are able to complete 11 reps or more, then you know you will need a heavier weight for the next set. If, on the other hand, you cannot complete a set of 10 repetitions, then the weight is too heavy and for the next set the poundage should be reduced. It may take two or three workouts (one to two weeks), to determine your exact max 10 rep. It is always better to find your max 10 rep by lift-ing a lighter weight and placing stress on the muscle fiber by increasing the number of repetitions than by trying to lift a weight that you cannot push even eight times. When you lift too heavy a weight, the risk of injury increases, especially to the connecting tissues (ligaments and tendons).

By causing the muscle to go to failure (unable to perform the lift), you have placed stress or an overload on the muscle fibers. The waste material, lactic acid, inhibits the muscle contractile system to respond to the requested work. It will take the lactic acid 30 to 45 seconds to break up, and then the exercise should be repeated. The muscle will adapt to the added weight/stress after it has repaired (usually 24 to 48 hours).

First set—80 percent of max 10 rep—
12 to 14 repetitions

Second set—100 percent of max 10 rep—
10 repetitions

Third set—80 percent of max 10 rep—
repetitions to fatigue

Order of Exercises

The exercises should be performed in the order that they are listed, from the largest muscle groups to the smallest ones. It is important to work the larger muscles first, as the smaller muscles are required for stability. When the larger muscles are worked, stress is placed on the smaller muscles. If the smaller muscles are fatigued, they are not able to assist in the movement for the larger muscles. For example, the bench press requires the use of the triceps muscle to assist in the lifting movement. If the triceps were fatigued, the pectoral muscle would have to perform on its own, but the triceps would inhibit the movement because it could not function to assist in the movement.

If you work the smaller muscle groups first, then when you work the larger muscle groups, the smaller muscles will reach failure before the large muscles are fatigued. The smaller muscles are the weak link and will not perform to assist the movement.

Weight Equipment

We have included free weights, weight machines, and the medicine ball in the program. Free weights are often the preferred option for weight lifting, as not only is it easy to adapt and alter exercises, but such factors as balance, increased range of movement, symmetrical development, muscle uniformity, and control are better satisfied with the use of free weights over machines. When using free weights, it is best to work with a partner and have someone spot or assist you when performing the exercise. This is especially important with high-risk exercises, such as any exercise where the weight has the potential of falling on the lifter. Since this workout includes lifting a weight to a max 10 rep in order to produce muscle failure, a spotter should be available to assist with the weight if needed. If there is not a spotter available and you are performing a high-risk exercise (e.g., the bench press), the weight being lifted and/or the number of repetitions being performed should be reduced. The muscle should not be taken to failure.

The use of weight machines with cable systems or self-spotting devices will allow you to perform an exercise to muscle failure if you are working out on your own. One drawback of weight machines, though, is they are built for one size of body and quite often cannot accommodate the smaller frame of many females and some males. Initially this does not pose a problem, but with repeated executions of an exercise, the range of motion, direction of execution, and joint integrity may be compromised.

The weight equipment (free or machines) at any gym should be studied, and choices should be made according to availability of a spotting partner, the fit of the machine to your body frame, and the desired outcome of the exercise.

When lifting, body position, the execution of the exercise, and breathing are important elements to remember. Exhale on effort, or when pressing the weight away from the starting position, and inhale on relaxation, or when returning the weight to the starting position. Find a comfortable rate of execution for you. It should not be too quick, because then the momentum of the weight, not your muscle power, will be carrying the limb to the end position. The execution should also not be too slow, as with boxing we are looking for a more explosive performance. Try to take the weight through the full range of motion, engaging a broad array of muscle fibers. Move the weight from the starting position in a controlled manner, pause, and then move it back to the finish position. The movement should be smooth and controlled. It is important to keep the body in the correct position as shown in the diagrams. The core should be tight, and all posture and supporting muscle should be in alignment so that the exercise may be executed correctly. This also reduces the chance of injury in the working muscle as well as in supporting muscles and joint regions.

Some Considerations

The weight that you are able to lift may vary from workout to workout. Some days you may feel stronger and be able to press more weight; other days you may feel fatigued before you even start. Extraneous conditions (such as health and personal commitments) can influence your workout capabilities. A reduced ability in lifting weights is often noticed during your first set. If during your first set you struggled to get 10 reps or did not even get 10 reps, reduce the weight for the second set. Do not forgo your workout; try to keep your schedule; just reduce the intensity and the workout time. Also, always be sure to start with a general warm-up to increase blood flow to the muscles. A three to five minute session of shadow boxing or jumping rope will prepare the muscles for lifting weights.

The Exercises with Weights

A combination of free weight exercises and machine exercises have been chosen for this program.

Lat Pull-Down

Weight machine. Targeted area: Back muscles—Latissimus Dorsi, Rhomboideus

Sit facing the weight machine. Hold the bar in an overhand wide grip, arms extended. Sit tall, leaning slightly back, chest lifted forward and knees steadied under the leg pads. Pull the bar down on angle toward the upper chest, and squeeze

the shoulder blades toward each other as you pull through. Pause and then return the weight to the starting position slowly and with control. Inhale as you bring the weight closer to the chest, and exhale as you release the bar away from the body. Focus on the back muscles, and allow the shoulders to go through a large range of motion.

Bench Press

Free weights or weight machine. Targeted area: Chest muscles— Pectorals

Lie on your back on a flat bench. Grasp the barbell in an overhand grip, slightly wider than shoulder-width apart. Press the bar straight up off the rack

Lat pull-down—start

Lat pull-down—finish

Bench press—start

Bench press—finish

Bent over dumbbell row—start

Bent over dumbbell row—finish

and over the chest area. Bend at the elbows and slowly lower the bar toward the middle of the chest, then press it straight up away from the chest without locking the elbows. Exhale on exertion (when pressing the weight into the air), and inhale when lowering the weight.

Bent Over Dumbbell Row

Free weights. Targeted area: Back muscles—Latissimus Dorsi, Rhomboideus

Place one knee on a flat bench. Lean forward with the body, hold a dumbbell in one hand, and place the other hand forward on the flat bench for torso support. Keep the back flat and the head in line with the back. Hold the weight in an overhand grip (knuckles forward) with the arm extended straight under the shoulder. Bring the shoulder blade toward the centerline of the body, then lift the elbow straight up toward the ceiling. The hand will rotate slightly with the knuckles facing out. There can also be a slight rotation of the body as the weight reaches shoulder height. Pause and slowly return the weight to the starting position. Ensure that the weight is lowered directly under the shoulder and not toward the back foot. Inhale as the weight is raised and exhale as the weight is lowered. Repeat with the other arm.

Seated pec deck—start

Seated Pec Deck

Weight machine. Targeted area: Chest muscles—Pectorals

Sit with the arms out at right angles (bent up at the elbows) at shoulder level and the forearms placed on the pads of the weight machine. Keep the back straight and the shoulders relaxed, and look straight ahead. Bring the arms together, contracting the center of the chest, and pulling from the elbow area, until the pads come together. Pause and then return the pads to the starting position. Exhale as the arms are brought together, and inhale as the arms open up toward the sides.

Standing Side Arm Raises

Free weights. Targeted area: Shoulders—Deltoids

Stand with feet hip-width apart and the knees relaxed. Extend the arms at the sides of the body and hold the weights with the knuckles facing out.

Seated pec deck—finish

Standing side arm raises—start

Raise the arms up to shoulder height laterally (out to the side of the body). Pause and then lower the arms slowly to the starting position. Hold the torso tight and initiate all movement from the shoulder region.

Triceps Pull-Down

Weight machine. Targeted area: Back of upper arm—Triceps

Stand, facing the machine. Hold the bar with both hands in an overhand close grip, chest level. Place the feet slightly less than hip-width apart, knees relaxed and torso tight. Keep the elbows close to the body and press the bar down toward the upper thighs until the arms are extended. Pause and slowly return the bar to the starting position, keeping the elbows at the sides of the body. Exhale as you press the bar down, and inhale as you release the bar.

Standing side arm raises—finish

Triceps pull-down—start

Triceps pull-down—finish

Seated Biceps Curl

Free weights. Targeted area: Front of upper arms—Biceps

Sit on a bench with the feet on the floor, the abdominals held tight, and the arms slightly bent at the elbow to maintain tension on the muscle. Extend the arms close to the sides of the body. Hold the dumbbell weights in an underhand grip, knuckles facing either forward or in toward the body. Keeping the torso strong and the elbows close to the body, raise the weights up toward the chest area. Pause at the top and lower the weights to starting position, stopping in front of the thighs.

Leg Extensions

Weight machine. Targeted area: Front of thigh—Quadriceps

Sit tall on the bench with the back supported and the thighs fully on the bench. Raise the lower legs slowly until they are extended. Pause at the top,

contract the quadriceps muscles, and then lower the legs slowly to the starting position. Be careful to not kick or swing the legs up. Do not allow the momentum of the weight to move the legs. Perform with a controlled movement. Exhale on lifting the legs, and inhale on lowering the legs.

Hamstring Curls

Weight machine. Targeted area: Back of thigh—Hamstrings

Lie facedown on the bench with the lower legs extended and the heels under the pads. Keep the knees slightly off the end of the bench. If the bench does not have a slight curve where the hip bones touch it, then place a towel under this area to assist in supporting the lower-back region. Hold onto the

Seated biceps curl—start

Seated biceps curl—finish

bench or stabilizing handles at the side of the bench, keeping the body straight and the hips on the bench. Slowly pull the heels toward the buttocks. Pause and then lower the legs to the starting position.

Abdominal Crunches

Targeted area: Front of the torso—Abdominus Recti

Lie on your back. Place your hands beside your head to give neck support, or cross your arms over your chest. Place both feet on the floor with the knees bent, or raise the knees over the hips. Contract the abdominal muscles, keeping the lower back on the floor. Exhale and lift the head and shoulders up off the ground as a unit and move toward the knees. Pause, and then lower the head and shoulders back toward the floor. Repeat, trying to lift closer to the knees each time. Continue until muscles feel fatigued, or up to three sets of 30 repetitions. (See photo on page 82.)

Oblique Crunches

Targeted area: Side of the torso—Obliques

Lie on your back as in the abdominal crunches. Lift the head and shoulders up off the floor and rotate to one side. Come back to center and lower back to the floor. Repeat on the other side. Repeat until muscles feel fatigued, or up to two sets of 20 repetitions. (See photo on page 83.)

Back Extensions

Targeted area: Lower back

Lie facedown. Extend the legs, and extend the arms overhead. Keep the torso on the floor. Hold the head in a straight line with the spine, and lift both legs and arms off the floor a few inches. Pause and lower the legs and arms to the floor. You may also lift one leg a time. Repeat until muscles feel fatigued, or up to two sets of 20 repetitions. (See photo on page 83.)

Leg extension—start

Leg extension—finish

Hamstring curls—start

Hamstring curls—finish

Abdominal crunches—start

Abdominal crunches—finish

Oblique crunches

Back extension—start

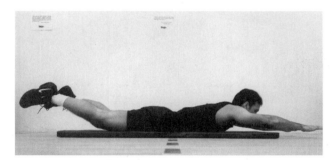

Back extension—finish

The Medicine Ball

From a boxer's point of view the medicine ball was designed to condition the abdominal muscles to absorb punishment. The best boxers know that their abdominals must be well armored against attack and follow the old-time boxing trainer's simple principle that the best way to prepare yourself to absorb blows to the stomach is to absorb blows to the stomach. In preparation for a bout, boxers throw the medicine ball to the abdominal region of a partner, varying the intensity of the throws, thus simulating a body attack. There are a variety of movements and exercises that use the medicine ball to strengthen the body core and abdominals without making direct contact with the torso. Ranging from 2 to 30 pounds, the medicine ball can offer a unique and effective workout, not only for the abdominal muscles, but also for the back, legs, shoulders, and arms. It allows for a greater range of motion when training the body core, as compared to weight machines, which can be restrictive, and free weights, which are not conducive to partner exchange movements.

The greatest advantage of using the medicine ball is that it trains the body core very effectively. It is often difficult to find exercises and training techniques that specifically challenge the main body, but with the use of the medicine ball, all of the torso's musculature is trained to respond to an overload simultaneously. When the medicine ball is tossed, all muscles must contract in order to catch the ball. The abdominal muscles and the back muscles are the two major areas of strength development. The muscles of the arms, chest, and legs can also be strengthened.

NOTE: The use of a medicine ball for abdominal strengthening should not even be considered until you feel comfortable performing a series of abdominal crunches and oblique exercises.

Medicine balls have gone through some changes in recent times. Traditionally black leather, they can now be found in various textures and filled with any number of different substances. We like how Dr. Donald Chu's "Plyoball" medicine ball performs. It is comfortable to hold, does not slip, and comes in a variety of sizes. Dr. Chu, a trainer of elite athletes, developed and successfully utilizes the medicine ball in his training.

The Exercises with the Medicine Ball

Basic Curl-Up

Lie on your back with knees bent and both feet on the floor. Hold the medicine ball on your chest. Control your upper body and head as one unit, and raise them off the floor until the ball touches your thigh. Return slowly to the floor. Repeat 10 to 20 times, one to three sets, 5-pound to 10-pound ball.

Pullover Sit-Up

Lie on your back with knees bent and both feet on the floor. Start with the arms fully extended on the floor overhead holding the ball. Bring the ball up overhead and forward toward the chest, and lift the upper body, head, and shoulders off the floor about 45 degrees. Return to the starting position, lowering the head and the ball to the floor at the same time. Repeat 10 to 15 times, one to three sets, 5-pound to 10-pound ball.

Hip Crunch

Sit on the floor with the knees bent and feet on the floor. Extend the arms behind the body and place the hands on the floor for support. Squeeze the ball between the knees. Raise the feet off the floor and pull the knees and ball toward the chest. Return the knees and feet to the starting position. Repeat 10 to 15 times, one to three sets, 5-pound to 10-pound ball.

Hip Raises

Lie on your back with your hands beside your head, legs extended straight over the hips, and the ball squeezed between the lower legs. Hold this position and lift the hips up and then lower back to the floor slowly and with control. Repeat 10 to 15 times, one to three sets, three-pound to five-pound ball.

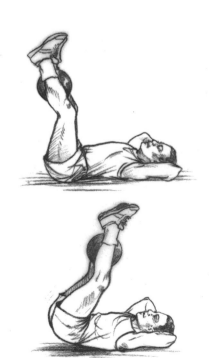

Oblique Twist

Lie on your back with the knees bent and both feet on the floor. Hold the medicine ball over the left shoulder area with both hands. Simultaneously lift the upper body and the ball up toward the right knee. Lower back slowly to the start position. Continue on one side for the full number of repetitions, and then repeat on the other side. Repeat 10 to 15 times, one to two sets, 5-pound to 10-pound ball.

Overhead Squat

Stand with the feet shoulder-width apart, and hold the ball at waist level. As you lower into a squat position, raise the medicine ball overhead. Keep the center of gravity over the heels, back straight, and head in line with the spine. Hold the squat position for two counts and return to the start. Repeat 10 to 15 times, one to three sets, 10-pound to 25-pound ball.

Sit-Up Toss (with a Partner)

Sit on the floor with the knees bent. Hold the arms extended in front of the body, ready to receive a ball toss from your partner. Start with your partner about five feet away. As you catch the ball, allow it to carry your arms backward and over your head. When the ball is above the head, lower the upper body toward the floor, keeping the arms extended. Sit up and toss the ball to your partner. Alternative toss: start with the arms bent in front of the body, catch the toss keeping the ball in front

Power Squat

Stand with the feet shoulder-width apart, and hold the ball in front of you close to the chest. As you lower into a squat position, keep the center of gravity over the heels, back straight, and head in line with the spine. Pause and then explode upward, extending the legs and pushing off the feet. Land on the floor in control rolling through the balls of the feet and attaining the squat position again. Pause and then jump again. Repeat 10 to 15 times, one to two sets, 10-pound to 25-pound ball.

of the body, and lower to the floor with control. Sit back up and toss the ball to your partner. Switch places with your partner. Repeat 10 to 15 times, one to two sets, 5-pound to 10-pound ball.

Partner Twist

Stand back-to-back with a partner. Rotate the body and pass the ball to your partner. To increase difficulty, increase the distance between you and your partner. Repeat 10 to 15 times, one to three sets, 5-pound to 10-pound ball.

Partner Standing Ball Toss

Stand facing your partner, and hold the ball overhead with the arms extended. While you step forward, toss the ball to your partner. Start about 6 to 10 feet apart and increase the distance to increase difficulty. Repeat 10 to 15 times, one to three sets, 5-pound to 10-pound ball.

Cool-Down Stretches

Refer to Chapter 7 and use these same stretches after your weight-lifting workout.

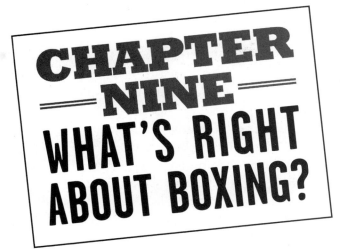

CHAPTER NINE
WHAT'S RIGHT ABOUT BOXING?

Three Minutes Never Seemed So Long!

I hear the bell. We touch gloves—this second never ends. This is the fight I've been waiting for. I stare my opponent down. Hear the roar of the crowd. Think about the game plan and keep my hands up. Protect the rib cage. The months of training. Keep looking at the target. Step away. A quick jab. Stick and move. Roll with the punches. A jab, another jab, and a straight right. Have to make a move and think about my combinations. Stay light on my feet. Get down lower and keep my balance. Hands up! Hands up! Slip and step away. Go in for the knockout! Slip and move. Ding! Ding! The bell sounds!

Boxing teaches you to rely on yourself, value the input of others, and respect both your own skills and those of others. It is rewarding and challenging; promotes athleticism, physical and mental conditioning, sportsmanship, and self-worth; and is one of the most challenging things that you ever do. Boxing is a great vehicle to release tension, stress, and frustrations, and it builds self-confidence and character. Amateur boxing is not about knocking your opponent out. It is about developing a skill, improving your fitness level, and setting goals.

For most, fitness boxing is enough. Hitting the heavy bag, working the speed bag, and skipping provide a challenging, creative way to stay fit and release stress. Some, however, may want to take it a step further and partake in controlled sparring. If you are ready for the next challenge, find a serious boxing club, start to work with a trainer, and get prepared to step into the ring.

Looking for a Boxing Club

Walking into a boxing club is experiencing, seeing, hearing, and smelling raw energy, and there really is nothing like it. The first thing that will catch your attention is the boxing ring. You'll notice the unique feeling of climbing through the ropes to shadow box and move around, the sound of the speed bag, the rhythmic pounding of the heavy bag, whirling hands and feet, and coaches yelling commands to their fighters. If you were not in the mood to work out before, you quickly get caught up in the atmosphere. Everyone has similar goals, and working hard is contagious.

Every club is different, but these are some basic things to look for. There should be a variety of heavy bags, double-end bags, and speed bags. Look for a conditioning area for both a cardiovascular workout and a muscle-conditioning workout, large mirrors to check your punching technique, a ring, target mitts, and boxing gloves. There should be changing facilities, times that are convenient to your workout schedule, and water available.

Many boxing clubs offer lessons for small groups, or you may prefer private instruction with a certified trainer or coach. Many fitness clubs now offer space for a good boxing noncontact workout, but serious boxing clubs dedicate space, a ring, equipment, and coaching specific to sparring and contact boxing.

Ensure that the feeling of the gym, the atmosphere, and the management are what you are looking for and that they seem like they'll be comfortable for you. The boxers training in the club should be concentrating, motivated, and hardworking. Club members should include both professionals and amateurs. The owners and trainers should be approachable and well informed about fitness training, boxing certification, rules, and regulations.

Sparring

Sparring should be done only in a controlled environment, with qualified supervision and with proper protective equipment. The first thing you must realize is that you will get hit (occasionally). Andy remembers his dad telling him, "Shadow box; practice your combinations on the heavy bag over and over until they become instinctive and automatic. Most boxers forget everything that they've learned the first time they get hit." "He

was right, I did!" Andy said. Everyone has a plan, until they get hit.

Find a serious boxing club, and spar under the supervision of an experienced, qualified boxing instructor. Protective equipment is necessary, and headgear, a mouthpiece, and a groin protector for males or chest protector for females must be worn. Sparring is done in the boxing ring, on a cushioned surface, and not on a hard floor surface. Both boxers wear 16-ounce gloves and listen and follow the coach's instructions.

Sparring allows you to practice offensive punches and introduces the defensive nature of the sport. You have to improvise your next move, and it is more complicated and intense than throwing punches on the heavy bag. Everything that you have practiced now has to be performed under pressure. The purpose of sparring is to fine-tune your skills and to simulate fight conditions in a controlled environment.

If you want to experience sparring, you have to be in great physical condition. You should be able to go three to four rounds on the heavy bag, run five to six miles, including sprints, and jump rope for at least 20 minutes. Before stepping into the ring and sparring, train at an intense level for 8 to 12 weeks, following a program like, the One-Two Punch Boxing Workout.

At a beginner level, your trainer will have you work with an experienced boxer who will not take advantage of your lack of experience. Early sparring sessions usually include one boxer working on defensive moves (deflecting and slipping punches), and the other working on offensive moves (throwing punches). The boxers then switch. At first, the offensive boxer throws only left jabs. There is a benefit for the defensive boxer to avoid just one type of punch, the left jab, and not worry about hooks or uppercuts or right-hand power shots. He or she can focus on the one punch and really work on slipping and moving. The trainer may switch roles and will add more elements into the sparring as the training continues.

What to Look for in a Trainer

A trainer should be certified with one of the national boxing associations and have experience training a successful boxer, whether it be an amateur or professional boxer. You want a trainer who knows the game inside and out and has a love of the sport.

Ensure that the trainer is approachable and listens to what you want so that a program can be designed for your needs. The trainer should be willing to share his or her successes and training beliefs freely and have enough time to commit to a training session at least once a week. A commitment from you is also necessary to work out in unsupervised sessions, doing roadwork, working the bag, and practicing what the trainer has taught you. Your commitment and the trainer's commitment are important so that your goals can be reached.

Watch a training session before you make your decision. Look for two-way communication between the trainer and the boxer, instruction that is clear, direct, patient, and consistent without a demeaning, reprimanding, or criticizing manner. A good trainer will bring out the best in you and place you on a schedule specific to your skill level and needs. He or she should identify your strengths and weaknesses and recognize that everyone progresses at his or her own rate.

Be honest with your trainer about your fitness level. This is especially important before each sparring session. Sparring is part of the training that requires good conditioning because of the possibility of getting hurt. If you have not been training or are not up to your normal physical condition, the trainer may delay the sparring session or adjust the intensity according to your physical condition.

The trainer will want to see your abilities and conditioning level before a decision will be made whether you are ready to spar. When the boxer feels ready and the trainer feels the boxer is ready, then a sparring match is set. Do not even think about sparring unless you have the conditioning. The trainer will pick sparring partners and oversee the sparring sessions. He or she will also ensure that the sparring is controlled and that an experienced boxer helps a less experienced boxer rather than taking advantage of the inexperience. Boxing training and sparring should be fun, not a struggle to keep from getting hurt.

Again, ensure that your trainer is qualified, has some successes, and knows and loves the sport. Many ex-boxers certainly know the sport and often make great trainers, but be aware that the expectations from the ex-boxer trainer may not be realistic. Patience can be lost if the new boxer is unable to grasp the moves and combinations as easily as the trainer once did. The ex-boxer trainer may try to mold the new boxer into a boxer just like he or she was, even though the new boxer has different strengths and weaknesses and the moves and combinations do not feel natural. Also, an ex-boxer trainer may be trying to relive his or her career through the new boxer.

Until the Last Bell

Fitness boxing is a demanding and exciting activity and is definitely an effective way to get into the best physical shape of your life. The 12-week program guides you through all the basics of fitness and teaches you how to go the distance to become more physically fit.

Take inventory of your life, and remember that the path you follow today is an investment in every day that is still to come. Whatever fitness activities you choose to be involved in, take pride in your performance, work the basics, and enjoy the journey. Give yourself time to adapt and grow, and make fitness a long-term, lifetime commitment, a regular part of your everyday life. Make fitness your personal journey.

Charting Your Progress

Your progression in The One-Two Punch Boxing Workout can be recorded in this 12-week logbook. By recording your training sessions on a daily basis, you will see how the benefits of performing the workouts result in an improved fitness level. Each week includes two days for the Boxer's Workout, two days for the Cardio-Conditioning Workout, two days for the Muscle Conditioning Workout, and one day for resting. Fill out the date and record the time or repetitions for each exercise performed that day.

Try not to miss a workout, especially the Boxer's Workout. If you must miss a workout, ensure that both Boxer's Workouts are performed and miss either the Cardio- or Muscle Conditioning days.

Tracking the Details

For the Boxer's Workout, refer to Chapter 6 for a quick summary of the amount of time and the intensity level that you spend on each of the exercises. Record the number of minutes you shadow boxed in the warm-up (between three and five min-

utes). Record the number of minutes that you jump rope. Remember that you want to work up to a twelve-minute jumping session, so if you are just starting out, record the jumping times and put the rest period in parentheses. For example, if you jump for five minutes, rest two minutes, and jump four minutes, this would give a total of nine minutes jumping and two minutes resting. It is recorded as 5(2)4.

For the next session—Shadow Boxing—record the time spent for each round, working up to three minutes for all the rounds. Choose the appropriate level of intensity, and record the number of minutes for each round on the heavy bag. Record the number of seconds for each sprint under Round 1, Round 2, Round 3, and Round 4. Using Target Mitts is an optional exercise, and you should record the number of minutes you hit the target mitts for each round. Try to work up to three rounds, each round three minutes long.

Choose a cool-down exercise—shadow boxing, double-end bag, or speed bag—and record the time performed. Ensure that your heart rate has decreased to within ten beats of your regular standing heart rate. Refer to Chapter 8 to choose the abdominal exercises and record the total number of repetitions. Refer to Chapter 7 for the stretching exercises and record the amount of time spent stretching.

For Cardio-Conditioning, refer to Chapter 7 and record the time spent warming up the muscles and elevating the heart rate. Record your running time under the Long Run category and add comments on how the run felt. Describe if the run was difficult or easy, or if you experienced any discomfort or pain, and at what point in the run this occurred. For the initial conditioning level, record the split time of walking and jogging as well as the total time. For example: walk (two minutes), jog (five minutes), and total time (twenty-three minutes) or 2/5/23. For the intermediate and advanced conditioning levels, record the continuous time spent running. If sprints were performed, record the length of the sprint time (twenty seconds) and the number of times the sprints were repeated, (four times) or 20/4. Also describe how the sprints felt. If you are unable to run or prefer to either jump rope or use a cardio-machine, then record the number of minutes that you trained jumping rope or working out on the cardio-machine. Record the number of minutes spent stretching the muscles and cooling down as described in Chapter 7.

Refer to Chapter 8 for the descriptions and explanations of the muscle conditioning exercises. Record the weight you are lifting and the number of repetitions for each exercise. For the abdominal crunch, oblique crunch, and back extension, record the number of repetitions completed for each exercise. For the Medicine Ball Exercises, record the total number of repetitions for all the exercises. Refer to Chapter 7 and record the time spent on stretching the muscles.

Keep It Going

Once you have completed the 12-week program, you can move up to the Champ's Workout—record the appropriate time and repetitions for these exercises. If you're short on time one day, you may want to perform the 30-Minute Maintenance Workout shown below. Just check off the exercises that you complete. To attain and maintain a great fitness level, make The One-Two Punch Boxing Workout a regular part of your life.

BOXING SHORTS
A 30-MINUTE MAINTENANCE WORKOUT

Warm-Up	3 minutes
Jump Rope	3 minutes
Heavy Bag	5 minutes
Jump Rope	5 minutes
Heavy Bag	5 minutes
Shadow Box	3 minutes
Abdominal Workout	4 minutes
Cool-Down/Stretches	2 minutes

The 12-Week Program Chart

WEEK 1

DAY 1   THE BOXER'S WORKOUT   DATE _____

	ROUND 1	ROUND 2	ROUND 3
Warm-Up			
Jump Rope			
Shadow Boxing			
Heavy Bag			
Heavy-Bag Speed Sprints			
Target Mitts (optional)			
Cool-Down Round			
Abdominal Workout			
Cool-Down/Stretches			

DAY 2   CARDIO-CONDITIONING   DATE _____

	TIME	DESCRIPTION
Warm-Up		
Long Run		
Running Sprints		
Jump Rope		
Cardio Machine		
Cool-Down/Stretches		

WEEK 1

DAY 3 — MUSCLE CONDITIONING   DATE _____

Warm-Up						
	Set 1		Set 2		Set 3	
	Wt	Reps	Wt	Reps	Wt	Reps
Lat Pull-Down						
Bench Press						
Bent-Over Dumbbell Row						
Seated Pec Deck						
Standing Side Arm Raises						
Triceps Pull-Down						
Seated Biceps Curl						
Leg Extensions						
Hamstring Curls						
Abdominal Crunches						
Oblique Crunches						
Back Extensions						
Medicine Ball Exercises						
Cool-Down/Stretches						

DAY 4 THE BOXER'S WORKOUT DATE _____

	ROUND 1	ROUND 2	ROUND 3
Warm-Up			
Jump Rope			
Shadow Boxing			
Heavy Bag			
Heavy-Bag Speed Sprints			
Target Mitts (optional)			
Cool-Down Round			
Abdominal Workout			
Cool-Down/Stretches			

DAY 5 CARDIO-CONDITIONING DATE _____

	TIME	DESCRIPTION
Warm-Up		
Long Run		
Running Sprints		
Jump Rope		
Cardio Machine		
Cool-Down/Stretches		

WEEK 1

DAY 6 MUSCLE CONDITIONING   DATE _____

Warm-Up						
	Set 1		Set 2		Set 3	
	Wt	Reps	Wt	Reps	Wt	Reps
Lat Pull-Down						
Bench Press						
Bent-Over Dumbbell Row						
Seated Pec Deck						
Standing Side Arm Raises						
Triceps Pull-Down						
Seated Biceps Curl						
Leg Extensions						
Hamstring Curls						
Abdominal Crunches						
Oblique Crunches						
Back Extensions						
Medicine Ball Exercises						
Cool-Down/Stretches						

DAY 7   REST   DATE _____

WEEK 2

DAY 1   THE BOXER'S WORKOUT   DATE _____

	ROUND 1	ROUND 2	ROUND 3
Warm-Up			
Jump Rope			
Shadow Boxing			
Heavy Bag			
Heavy-Bag Speed Sprints			
Target Mitts (optional)			
Cool-Down Round			
Abdominal Workout			
Cool-Down/Stretches			

DAY 2   CARDIO-CONDITIONING   DATE _____

	TIME	DESCRIPTION
Warm-Up		
Long Run		
Running Sprints		
Jump Rope		
Cardio Machine		
Cool-Down/Stretches		

WEEK 2

DAY 3 — MUSCLE CONDITIONING DATE _____

Warm-Up						
	Set 1		Set 2		Set 3	
	Wt	Reps	Wt	Reps	Wt	Reps
Lat Pull-Down						
Bench Press						
Bent-Over Dumbbell Row						
Seated Pec Deck						
Standing Side Arm Raises						
Triceps Pull-Down						
Seated Biceps Curl						
Leg Extensions						
Hamstring Curls						
Abdominal Crunches						
Oblique Crunches						
Back Extensions						
Medicine Ball Exercises						
Cool-Down/Stretches						

DAY 4　THE BOXER'S WORKOUT　DATE _____

	ROUND 1	ROUND 2	ROUND 3
Warm-Up			
Jump Rope			
Shadow Boxing			
Heavy Bag			
Heavy-Bag Speed Sprints			
Target Mitts (optional)			
Cool-Down Round			
Abdominal Workout			
Cool-Down/Stretches			

DAY 5　CARDIO-CONDITIONING　DATE _____

	TIME	DESCRIPTION
Warm-Up		
Long Run		
Running Sprints		
Jump Rope		
Cardio Machine		
Cool-Down/Stretches		

WEEK 2

DAY 6   MUSCLE CONDITIONING   DATE _____

Warm-Up						
	Set 1		Set 2		Set 3	
	Wt	Reps	Wt	Reps	Wt	Reps
Lat Pull-Down						
Bench Press						
Bent-Over Dumbbell Row						
Seated Pec Deck						
Standing Side Arm Raises						
Triceps Pull-Down						
Seated Biceps Curl						
Leg Extensions						
Hamstring Curls						
Abdominal Crunches						
Oblique Crunches						
Back Extensions						
Medicine Ball Exercises						
Cool-Down/Stretches						

DAY 7   REST   DATE _____

WEEK 3

DAY 1   THE BOXER'S WORKOUT   DATE _____

	ROUND 1	ROUND 2	ROUND 3
Warm-Up			
Jump Rope			
Shadow Boxing			
Heavy Bag			
Heavy-Bag Speed Sprints			
Target Mitts (optional)			
Cool-Down Round			
Abdominal Workout			
Cool-Down/Stretches			

DAY 2   CARDIO-CONDITIONING   DATE _____

	TIME	DESCRIPTION
Warm-Up		
Long Run		
Running Sprints		
Jump Rope		
Cardio Machine		
Cool-Down/Stretches		

WEEK 3

DAY 3 — MUSCLE CONDITIONING — DATE _____

Warm-Up						
	Set 1		Set 2		Set 3	
	Wt	Reps	Wt	Reps	Wt	Reps
Lat Pull-Down						
Bench Press						
Bent-Over Dumbbell Row						
Seated Pec Deck						
Standing Side Arm Raises						
Triceps Pull-Down						
Seated Biceps Curl						
Leg Extensions						
Hamstring Curls						
Abdominal Crunches						
Oblique Crunches						
Back Extensions						
Medicine Ball Exercises						
Cool-Down/Stretches						

DAY 4 THE BOXER'S WORKOUT DATE _____

	ROUND 1	ROUND 2	ROUND 3
Warm-Up			
Jump Rope			
Shadow Boxing			
Heavy Bag			
Heavy-Bag Speed Sprints			
Target Mitts (optional)			
Cool-Down Round			
Abdominal Workout			
Cool-Down/Stretches			

DAY 5 CARDIO-CONDITIONING DATE _____

	TIME	DESCRIPTION
Warm-Up		
Long Run		
Running Sprints		
Jump Rope		
Cardio Machine		
Cool-Down/Stretches		

WEEK 3

DAY 6 — MUSCLE CONDITIONING — DATE _____

Warm-Up						
	Set 1		Set 2		Set 3	
	Wt	Reps	Wt	Reps	Wt	Reps
Lat Pull-Down						
Bench Press						
Bent-Over Dumbbell Row						
Seated Pec Deck						
Standing Side Arm Raises						
Triceps Pull-Down						
Seated Biceps Curl						
Leg Extensions						
Hamstring Curls						
Abdominal Crunches						
Oblique Crunches						
Back Extensions						
Medicine Ball Exercises						
Cool-Down/Stretches						

DAY 7 — REST — DATE _____

WEEK 4

DAY 1 — THE BOXER'S WORKOUT   DATE _____

	ROUND 1	ROUND 2	ROUND 3
Warm-Up			
Jump Rope			
Shadow Boxing			
Heavy Bag			
Heavy-Bag Speed Sprints			
Target Mitts (optional)			
Cool-Down Round			
Abdominal Workout			
Cool-Down/Stretches			

DAY 2 — CARDIO-CONDITIONING   DATE _____

	TIME	DESCRIPTION
Warm-Up		
Long Run		
Running Sprints		
Jump Rope		
Cardio Machine		
Cool-Down/Stretches		

WEEK 4

DAY 3 | MUSCLE CONDITIONING   DATE _____

Warm-Up						
	Set 1		Set 2		Set 3	
	Wt	Reps	Wt	Reps	Wt	Reps
Lat Pull-Down						
Bench Press						
Bent-Over Dumbbell Row						
Seated Pec Deck						
Standing Side Arm Raises						
Triceps Pull-Down						
Seated Biceps Curl						
Leg Extensions						
Hamstring Curls						
Abdominal Crunches						
Oblique Crunches						
Back Extensions						
Medicine Ball Exercises						
Cool-Down/Stretches						

DAY 4 THE BOXER'S WORKOUT DATE _____

	ROUND 1	ROUND 2	ROUND 3
Warm-Up			
Jump Rope			
Shadow Boxing			
Heavy Bag			
Heavy-Bag Speed Sprints			
Target Mitts (optional)			
Cool-Down Round			
Abdominal Workout			
Cool-Down/Stretches			

DAY 5 CARDIO-CONDITIONING DATE _____

	TIME	DESCRIPTION
Warm-Up		
Long Run		
Running Sprints		
Jump Rope		
Cardio Machine		
Cool-Down/Stretches		

WEEK 4

DAY 6   MUSCLE CONDITIONING   DATE _____

Warm-Up						
	Set 1		Set 2		Set 3	
	Wt	Reps	Wt	Reps	Wt	Reps
Lat Pull-Down						
Bench Press						
Bent-Over Dumbbell Row						
Seated Pec Deck						
Standing Side Arm Raises						
Triceps Pull-Down						
Seated Biceps Curl						
Leg Extensions						
Hamstring Curls						
Abdominal Crunches						
Oblique Crunches						
Back Extensions						
Medicine Ball Exercises						
Cool-Down/Stretches						

DAY 7   REST   DATE _____

WEEK 5

DAY 1 — THE BOXER'S WORKOUT   DATE _____

Warm-Up			
Jump Rope			
	ROUND 1	ROUND 2	ROUND 3
Shadow Boxing			
Heavy Bag			
Heavy-Bag Speed Sprints			
Target Mitts (optional)			
Cool-Down Round			
Abdominal Workout			
Cool-Down/Stretches			

DAY 2 — CARDIO-CONDITIONING   DATE _____

	TIME	DESCRIPTION
Warm-Up		
Long Run		
Running Sprints		
Jump Rope		
Cardio Machine		
Cool-Down/Stretches		

WEEK 5

DAY 3 MUSCLE CONDITIONING   DATE _____

Warm-Up						
	Set 1		Set 2		Set 3	
	Wt	Reps	Wt	Reps	Wt	Reps
Lat Pull-Down						
Bench Press						
Bent-Over Dumbbell Row						
Seated Pec Deck						
Standing Side Arm Raises						
Triceps Pull-Down						
Seated Biceps Curl						
Leg Extensions						
Hamstring Curls						
Abdominal Crunches						
Oblique Crunches						
Back Extensions						
Medicine Ball Exercises						
Cool-Down/Stretches						

DAY 4 — THE BOXER'S WORKOUT   DATE _____

Warm-Up			
Jump Rope			
	ROUND 1	ROUND 2	ROUND 3
Shadow Boxing			
Heavy Bag			
Heavy-Bag Speed Sprints			
Target Mitts (optional)			
Cool-Down Round			
Abdominal Workout			
Cool-Down/Stretches			

DAY 5 — CARDIO-CONDITIONING   DATE _____

	TIME	DESCRIPTION
Warm-Up		
Long Run		
Running Sprints		
Jump Rope		
Cardio Machine		
Cool-Down/Stretches		

WEEK 5

DAY 6 — MUSCLE CONDITIONING   DATE _____

Warm-Up	Set 1		Set 2		Set 3	
	Wt	Reps	Wt	Reps	Wt	Reps
Lat Pull-Down						
Bench Press						
Bent-Over Dumbbell Row						
Seated Pec Deck						
Standing Side Arm Raises						
Triceps Pull-Down						
Seated Biceps Curl						
Leg Extensions						
Hamstring Curls						
Abdominal Crunches						
Oblique Crunches						
Back Extensions						
Medicine Ball Exercises						
Cool-Down/Stretches						

DAY 7   REST   DATE _____

WEEK 6

DAY 1 THE BOXER'S WORKOUT DATE _____

Warm-Up			
Jump Rope			
	ROUND 1	**ROUND 2**	**ROUND 3**
Shadow Boxing			
Heavy Bag			
Heavy-Bag Speed Sprints			
Target Mitts (optional)			
Cool-Down Round			
Abdominal Workout			
Cool-Down/Stretches			

DAY 2 CARDIO-CONDITIONING DATE _____

	TIME	**DESCRIPTION**
Warm-Up		
Long Run		
Running Sprints		
Jump Rope		
Cardio Machine		
Cool-Down/Stretches		

WEEK 6

DAY 3 MUSCLE CONDITIONING DATE _____

Warm-Up						
	Set 1		Set 2		Set 3	
	Wt	Reps	Wt	Reps	Wt	Reps
Lat Pull-Down						
Bench Press						
Bent-Over Dumbbell Row						
Seated Pec Deck						
Standing Side Arm Raises						
Triceps Pull-Down						
Seated Biceps Curl						
Leg Extensions						
Hamstring Curls						
Abdominal Crunches						
Oblique Crunches						
Back Extensions						
Medicine Ball Exercises						
Cool-Down/Stretches						

DAY 4 THE BOXER'S WORKOUT   DATE _____

	ROUND 1	ROUND 2	ROUND 3
Warm-Up			
Jump Rope			
Shadow Boxing			
Heavy Bag			
Heavy-Bag Speed Sprints			
Target Mitts (optional)			
Cool-Down Round			
Abdominal Workout			
Cool-Down/Stretches			

DAY 5 CARDIO-CONDITIONING   DATE _____

	TIME	DESCRIPTION
Warm-Up		
Long Run		
Running Sprints		
Jump Rope		
Cardio Machine		
Cool-Down/Stretches		

WEEK 6

DAY 6 — MUSCLE CONDITIONING — DATE _____

Warm-Up						
	Set 1		Set 2		Set 3	
	Wt	Reps	Wt	Reps	Wt	Reps
Lat Pull-Down						
Bench Press						
Bent-Over Dumbbell Row						
Seated Pec Deck						
Standing Side Arm Raises						
Triceps Pull-Down						
Seated Biceps Curl						
Leg Extensions						
Hamstring Curls						
Abdominal Crunches						
Oblique Crunches						
Back Extensions						
Medicine Ball Exercises						
Cool-Down/Stretches						

DAY 7 — REST — DATE _____

WEEK 7

DAY 1 THE BOXER'S WORKOUT DATE _____

	ROUND 1	ROUND 2	ROUND 3
Warm-Up			
Jump Rope			
Shadow Boxing			
Heavy Bag			
Heavy-Bag Speed Sprints			
Target Mitts (optional)			
Cool-Down Round			
Abdominal Workout			
Cool-Down/Stretches			

DAY 2 CARDIO-CONDITIONING DATE _____

	TIME	DESCRIPTION
Warm-Up		
Long Run		
Running Sprints		
Jump Rope		
Cardio Machine		
Cool-Down/Stretches		

WEEK 7

DAY 3 MUSCLE CONDITIONING DATE _____

Warm-Up						
	Set 1		Set 2		Set 3	
	Wt	Reps	Wt	Reps	Wt	Reps
Lat Pull-Down						
Bench Press						
Bent-Over Dumbbell Row						
Seated Pec Deck						
Standing Side Arm Raises						
Triceps Pull-Down						
Seated Biceps Curl						
Leg Extensions						
Hamstring Curls						
Abdominal Crunches						
Oblique Crunches						
Back Extensions						
Medicine Ball Exercises						
Cool-Down/Stretches						

DAY 4 — THE BOXER'S WORKOUT DATE _____

	ROUND 1	ROUND 2	ROUND 3
Warm-Up			
Jump Rope			
Shadow Boxing			
Heavy Bag			
Heavy-Bag Speed Sprints			
Target Mitts (optional)			
Cool-Down Round			
Abdominal Workout			
Cool-Down/Stretches			

DAY 5 — CARDIO-CONDITIONING DATE _____

	TIME	DESCRIPTION
Warm-Up		
Long Run		
Running Sprints		
Jump Rope		
Cardio Machine		
Cool-Down/Stretches		

WEEK 7

DAY 6 MUSCLE CONDITIONING DATE _____

Warm-Up						
	Set 1		Set 2		Set 3	
	Wt	Reps	Wt	Reps	Wt	Reps
Lat Pull-Down						
Bench Press						
Bent-Over Dumbbell Row						
Seated Pec Deck						
Standing Side Arm Raises						
Triceps Pull-Down						
Seated Biceps Curl						
Leg Extensions						
Hamstring Curls						
Abdominal Crunches						
Oblique Crunches						
Back Extensions						
Medicine Ball Exercises						
Cool-Down/Stretches						

DAY 7 REST DATE _____

WEEK 8

DAY 1   THE BOXER'S WORKOUT   DATE _____

	ROUND 1	ROUND 2	ROUND 3
Warm-Up			
Jump Rope			
Shadow Boxing			
Heavy Bag			
Heavy-Bag Speed Sprints			
Target Mitts (optional)			
Cool-Down Round			
Abdominal Workout			
Cool-Down/Stretches			

DAY 2   CARDIO-CONDITIONING   DATE _____

	TIME	DESCRIPTION
Warm-Up		
Long Run		
Running Sprints		
Jump Rope		
Cardio Machine		
Cool-Down/Stretches		

WEEK 8

DAY 3 MUSCLE CONDITIONING   DATE _____

Warm-Up						
	Set 1		Set 2		Set 3	
	Wt	Reps	Wt	Reps	Wt	Reps
Lat Pull-Down						
Bench Press						
Bent-Over Dumbbell Row						
Seated Pec Deck						
Standing Side Arm Raises						
Triceps Pull-Down						
Seated Biceps Curl						
Leg Extensions						
Hamstring Curls						
Abdominal Crunches						
Oblique Crunches						
Back Extensions						
Medicine Ball Exercises						
Cool-Down/Stretches						

DAY 4 · THE BOXER'S WORKOUT DATE _____

	ROUND 1	ROUND 2	ROUND 3
Warm-Up			
Jump Rope			
Shadow Boxing			
Heavy Bag			
Heavy-Bag Speed Sprints			
Target Mitts (optional)			
Cool-Down Round			
Abdominal Workout			
Cool-Down/Stretches			

DAY 5 · CARDIO-CONDITIONING DATE _____

	TIME	DESCRIPTION
Warm-Up		
Long Run		
Running Sprints		
Jump Rope		
Cardio Machine		
Cool-Down/Stretches		

WEEK 8

DAY 6　MUSCLE CONDITIONING　DATE _____

Warm-Up						
	Set 1		Set 2		Set 3	
	Wt	Reps	Wt	Reps	Wt	Reps
Lat Pull-Down						
Bench Press						
Bent-Over Dumbbell Row						
Seated Pec Deck						
Standing Side Arm Raises						
Triceps Pull-Down						
Seated Biceps Curl						
Leg Extensions						
Hamstring Curls						
Abdominal Crunches						
Oblique Crunches						
Back Extensions						
Medicine Ball Exercises						
Cool-Down/Stretches						

DAY 7　REST　DATE _____

WEEK 9

DAY 1 — THE BOXER'S WORKOUT   DATE _____

	ROUND 1	ROUND 2	ROUND 3
Warm-Up			
Jump Rope			
Shadow Boxing			
Heavy Bag			
Heavy-Bag Speed Sprints			
Target Mitts (optional)			
Cool-Down Round			
Abdominal Workout			
Cool-Down/Stretches			

DAY 2 — CARDIO-CONDITIONING   DATE _____

	TIME	DESCRIPTION
Warm-Up		
Long Run		
Running Sprints		
Jump Rope		
Cardio Machine		
Cool-Down/Stretches		

WEEK 9

DAY 3 MUSCLE CONDITIONING DATE _____

Warm-Up						
	Set 1		Set 2		Set 3	
	Wt	Reps	Wt	Reps	Wt	Reps
Lat Pull-Down						
Bench Press						
Bent-Over Dumbbell Row						
Seated Pec Deck						
Standing Side Arm Raises						
Triceps Pull-Down						
Seated Biceps Curl						
Leg Extensions						
Hamstring Curls						
Abdominal Crunches						
Oblique Crunches						
Back Extensions						
Medicine Ball Exercises						
Cool-Down/Stretches						

DAY 4 — THE BOXER'S WORKOUT   DATE _____

	ROUND 1	ROUND 2	ROUND 3
Warm-Up			
Jump Rope			
Shadow Boxing			
Heavy Bag			
Heavy-Bag Speed Sprints			
Target Mitts (optional)			
Cool-Down Round			
Abdominal Workout			
Cool-Down/Stretches			

DAY 5 — CARDIO-CONDITIONING   DATE _____

	TIME	DESCRIPTION
Warm-Up		
Long Run		
Running Sprints		
Jump Rope		
Cardio Machine		
Cool-Down/Stretches		

WEEK 9

DAY 6   MUSCLE CONDITIONING   DATE _____

Warm-Up						
	Set 1		Set 2		Set 3	
	Wt	Reps	Wt	Reps	Wt	Reps
Lat Pull-Down						
Bench Press						
Bent-Over Dumbbell Row						
Seated Pec Deck						
Standing Side Arm Raises						
Triceps Pull-Down						
Seated Biceps Curl						
Leg Extensions						
Hamstring Curls						
Abdominal Crunches						
Oblique Crunches						
Back Extensions						
Medicine Ball Exercises						
Cool-Down/Stretches						

DAY 7   REST   DATE _____

WEEK 10

DAY 1 — THE BOXER'S WORKOUT   DATE _____

	ROUND 1	ROUND 2	ROUND 3
Warm-Up			
Jump Rope			
Shadow Boxing			
Heavy Bag			
Heavy-Bag Speed Sprints			
Target Mitts (optional)			
Cool-Down Round			
Abdominal Workout			
Cool-Down/Stretches			

DAY 2 — CARDIO-CONDITIONING   DATE _____

	TIME	DESCRIPTION
Warm-Up		
Long Run		
Running Sprints		
Jump Rope		
Cardio Machine		
Cool-Down/Stretches		

WEEK 10

DAY 3 MUSCLE CONDITIONING   DATE _____

Warm-Up						
	Set 1		Set 2		Set 3	
	Wt	Reps	Wt	Reps	Wt	Reps
Lat Pull-Down						
Bench Press						
Bent-Over Dumbbell Row						
Seated Pec Deck						
Standing Side Arm Raises						
Triceps Pull-Down						
Seated Biceps Curl						
Leg Extensions						
Hamstring Curls						
Abdominal Crunches						
Oblique Crunches						
Back Extensions						
Medicine Ball Exercises						
Cool-Down/Stretches						

DAY 4   THE BOXER'S WORKOUT   DATE _____

	ROUND 1	ROUND 2	ROUND 3
Warm-Up			
Jump Rope			
Shadow Boxing			
Heavy Bag			
Heavy-Bag Speed Sprints			
Target Mitts (optional)			
Cool-Down Round			
Abdominal Workout			
Cool-Down/Stretches			

DAY 5   CARDIO-CONDITIONING   DATE _____

	TIME	DESCRIPTION
Warm-Up		
Long Run		
Running Sprints		
Jump Rope		
Cardio Machine		
Cool-Down/Stretches		

WEEK 10

DAY 6 MUSCLE CONDITIONING DATE _____

Warm-Up						
	Set 1		**Set 2**		**Set 3**	
	Wt	**Reps**	**Wt**	**Reps**	**Wt**	**Reps**
Lat Pull-Down						
Bench Press						
Bent-Over Dumbbell Row						
Seated Pec Deck						
Standing Side Arm Raises						
Triceps Pull-Down						
Seated Biceps Curl						
Leg Extensions						
Hamstring Curls						
Abdominal Crunches						
Oblique Crunches						
Back Extensions						
Medicine Ball Exercises						
Cool-Down/Stretches						

DAY 7   REST   DATE _____

WEEK 11

DAY 1   THE BOXER'S WORKOUT   DATE _____

	ROUND 1	ROUND 2	ROUND 3
Warm-Up			
Jump Rope			
Shadow Boxing			
Heavy Bag			
Heavy-Bag Speed Sprints			
Target Mitts (optional)			
Cool-Down Round			
Abdominal Workout			
Cool-Down/Stretches			

DAY 2   CARDIO-CONDITIONING   DATE _____

	TIME	DESCRIPTION
Warm-Up		
Long Run		
Running Sprints		
Jump Rope		
Cardio Machine		
Cool-Down/Stretches		

WEEK 11

DAY 3 MUSCLE CONDITIONING DATE _____

Warm-Up						
	Set 1		Set 2		Set 3	
	Wt	Reps	Wt	Reps	Wt	Reps
Lat Pull-Down						
Bench Press						
Bent-Over Dumbbell Row						
Seated Pec Deck						
Standing Side Arm Raises						
Triceps Pull-Down						
Seated Biceps Curl						
Leg Extensions						
Hamstring Curls						
Abdominal Crunches						
Oblique Crunches						
Back Extensions						
Medicine Ball Exercises						
Cool-Down/Stretches						

DAY 4   THE BOXER'S WORKOUT   DATE _____

	ROUND 1	ROUND 2	ROUND 3
Warm-Up			
Jump Rope			
Shadow Boxing			
Heavy Bag			
Heavy-Bag Speed Sprints			
Target Mitts (optional)			
Cool-Down Round			
Abdominal Workout			
Cool-Down/Stretches			

DAY 5   CARDIO-CONDITIONING   DATE _____

	TIME	DESCRIPTION
Warm-Up		
Long Run		
Running Sprints		
Jump Rope		
Cardio Machine		
Cool-Down/Stretches		

WEEK 11

DAY 6 MUSCLE CONDITIONING DATE _____

Warm-Up	Set 1		Set 2		Set 3	
	Wt	Reps	Wt	Reps	Wt	Reps
Lat Pull-Down						
Bench Press						
Bent-Over Dumbbell Row						
Seated Pec Deck						
Standing Side Arm Raises						
Triceps Pull-Down						
Seated Biceps Curl						
Leg Extensions						
Hamstring Curls						
Abdominal Crunches						
Oblique Crunches						
Back Extensions						
Medicine Ball Exercises						
Cool-Down/Stretches						

DAY 7 REST DATE _____

WEEK 12

DAY 1 THE BOXER'S WORKOUT   DATE _____

	ROUND 1	ROUND 2	ROUND 3
Warm-Up			
Jump Rope			
Shadow Boxing			
Heavy Bag			
Heavy-Bag Speed Sprints			
Target Mitts (optional)			
Cool-Down Round			
Abdominal Workout			
Cool-Down/Stretches			

DAY 2 CARDIO-CONDITIONING   DATE _____

	TIME	DESCRIPTION
Warm-Up		
Long Run		
Running Sprints		
Jump Rope		
Cardio Machine		
Cool-Down/Stretches		

WEEK 12

DAY 3   MUSCLE CONDITIONING   DATE _____

Warm-Up						
	Set 1		Set 2		Set 3	
	Wt	Reps	Wt	Reps	Wt	Reps
Lat Pull-Down						
Bench Press						
Bent-Over Dumbbell Row						
Seated Pec Deck						
Standing Side Arm Raises						
Triceps Pull-Down						
Seated Biceps Curl						
Leg Extensions						
Hamstring Curls						
Abdominal Crunches						
Oblique Crunches						
Back Extensions						
Medicine Ball Exercises						
Cool-Down/Stretches						

DAY 4 THE BOXER'S WORKOUT   DATE _____

	ROUND 1	ROUND 2	ROUND 3
Warm-Up			
Jump Rope			
Shadow Boxing			
Heavy Bag			
Heavy-Bag Speed Sprints			
Target Mitts (optional)			
Cool-Down Round			
Abdominal Workout			
Cool-Down/Stretches			

DAY 5 CARDIO-CONDITIONING   DATE _____

	TIME	DESCRIPTION
Warm-Up		
Long Run		
Running Sprints		
Jump Rope		
Cardio Machine		
Cool-Down/Stretches		

WEEK 12

DAY 6 — MUSCLE CONDITIONING   DATE _____

Warm-Up	Set 1		Set 2		Set 3	
	Wt	Reps	Wt	Reps	Wt	Reps
Lat Pull-Down						
Bench Press						
Bent-Over Dumbbell Row						
Seated Pec Deck						
Standing Side Arm Raises						
Triceps Pull-Down						
Seated Biceps Curl						
Leg Extensions						
Hamstring Curls						
Abdominal Crunches						
Oblique Crunches						
Back Extensions						
Medicine Ball Exercises						
Cool-Down/Stretches						

DAY 7   REST   DATE _____

THE CHAMP'S WORKOUT

Warm-Up

Jump Rope
  Warm-up: easy jumping 2 minutes
  Normal jumping 2 to 4 minutes
  Sprints: 20 double jumps
  Normal jumping 2 to 4 minutes

  Sprints: 30 double jumps
  Normal jumping 2 to 4 minutes
  Sprints: 40 double jumps
  Cool down: easy jumping 2 to 4 minutes

Shadow Boxing (with weights)
  Round 1: Basic punches
  Round 2: Combinations with head movement and fluidity
  Round 3: Combinations with head and foot movement
  Round 4: No weights, increase intensity, combinations, footwork

Heavy Bag Speed Sprints
  Sprint 40 seconds   Rest 40 seconds
  Sprint 40 seconds   Rest 40 seconds
  Sprint 30 seconds   Rest 30 seconds
  Sprint 30 seconds   Rest 30 seconds
  Sprint 20 seconds   Rest 20 seconds
  Sprint 20 seconds   Rest 20 seconds

Heavy bag 3 minute rounds
  Round 1: Mixed punches, footwork, combinations at high intensity, then rest 1 minute.
  Round 2: Mixed punches, footwork, combinations at high intensity, then rest 1 minute.
  Round 3: Mixed punches, footwork, combinations at high intensity, then rest 1 minute.
  Round 4: Mixed punches, footwork, combinations at high intensity, then rest 1 minute.

Target Mitts 3 minute rounds (Optional)
  Round 1: With a partner. Concentrate on punches.
  Round 2: With a partner. Concentrate on punches.
  Round 3: With a partner. Concentrate on punches.

Cool-Down Round
  Speed bag 3 minutes
  Double-end bag 3 minutes
  Shadow box (lightly) 3 minutes

Abdominal Workout

Cool-Down/Stretches

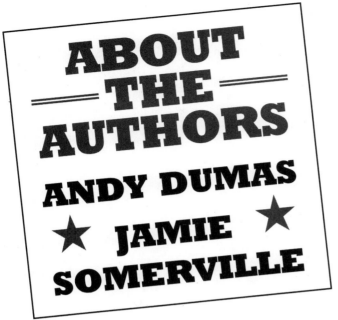

ABOUT THE AUTHORS
ANDY DUMAS ★ JAMIE SOMERVILLE

Andy Dumas is one of Canada's leading fitness experts. Born into a boxing background, he had the fortune of growing up in an environment that promoted physical activity. At a young age he hit the heavy bag, worked on his rhythm on the speed bag, jumped rope, and learned to move around the ring. As a Canadian boxing coach and certified fitness consultant, he understands the long hours of training, the commitment to the sport, and the intense mental focus that is required by the very best conditioned athlete.

Along with his partner Jamie Somerville, he is the cocreator of the highly successful workout video "The One-Two Punch." As a sought-after fitness presenter, he has been featured at major fitness conferences and various educational facilities, and he has appeared on many TV and radio programs.

Dumas promotes cross training and believes fitness is essential to good living. He lives, writes, teaches, and works out in Oakville, Ontario, Canada.

Jamie Somerville is a firm believer that fitness is for absolutely everyone. With an honors bachelor of science degree in human kinetics from the University of Waterloo, Ontario, Canada, she has extensive experience in the fitness industry, managing fitness centers, and providing personal training. She is a trainer of fitness instructors and develops and implements a variety of programs and workshops for fitness clubs.

Somerville started her involvement in physical activity with ballet and continues to undertake the challenges of this pursuit along with the demands of boxing training. She divides her time between writing, developing new workout videos, and laughing with her two daughters.